CW00492516

SECONDHAND AND VINTAGE

PARIS

Natasha Edwards

Vivays Publishing

Special thanks to my daughter Olivia, who visited
numerous vintage boutiques with me and even tried
some of the clothes on, to Jean-Pierre, who is as addicted
to the *brocantes* and flea markets as I am, and to Marie-
Claire Bordaz, who shared the task of taking photographs
for this book, as well as to the different shopkeepers and
stallholders who shared their enthusiasm and vintage finds.

Published by Vivays Publishing Ltd

www.vivays-publishing.com

© 2013 Natasha Edwards

A catalogue record for this book is
available from the British Library.

ISBN 978-1-908126-29-0

Publishing Director: Lee Ripley
Editor: Andrew Whittaker
Design: Draught Associates
Cover image: TessandJess.wordpress.com/2012/03/18/paris
Map data: © OpenStreetMap (and) contributors, CC-BY-SA

Printed in China

PARIS
CONTENTS

PARIS
HOW TO USE THIS BOOK

Each chapter in *Secondhand and Vintage Paris* has a theme. The first three are categorised by goods – Clothes & Accessories; Books, Music & Memorabilia; and Home & Interiors. Chapter four, Only in Paris, covers the flea markets, auctions, *brocantes* and more.

The entries within the first three chapters are arranged by location; in chapter four the main focus is on the different arcades making up the Marché aux Puces de Saint-Ouen (Clignancourt), Paris' largest flea market, but also moves around the wider city to visit other markets, shops and events. Each entry includes a description of the shop or market, alongside contact details, opening times and a guide to the relative price of the goods, set on a scale from € to €€€ (from bargain to investment).

A section of maps in the second half of the book shows you where to find the shops and markets, with each trader marked by a coloured diamond. The colour of the diamonds on the maps corresponds to the chapter colourings. The maps also feature a QR link, enabling you to access each one using a smartphone.

INTRODUCTION

All the different facets of the French capital are reflected in its secondhand offerings: the long tradition of crafts-manship in hundreds of years' worth of furniture and decorative items; the intellectual capital, descendant of the Enlightenment with its publishers, film-makers, photographers, cartoonists and *bouquinistes*; the fashion magnet with its haute couture tradition and legendary fashion labels.

Of course there have been Parisian collectors for generations, and the Surrealists enthused about the flea markets back in the 1920s and 30s, yet there's no doubt that the past few years have seen an explosion and transformation of Paris' secondhand outlets, from the clutter of anything goes *dépôt ventes* to carefully curated vintage stores and galleries. Take classic modern furniture design of the 1950s and 60s, a meeting of industrial design, avant-garde creativity and France's long decorative arts tradition, where yesterday's discarded junk has become art collectors' and investors' treasures (and often much more expensive now than what are still considered 'real' antiques) presented in galleries, while other stores salvage sofas, coffee pots and tea towels in a cheerful image of 60s domestic bliss. Clothes stores show a split between places where you might be buying hand-stitched items or the designer labels that have perhaps made fashion history, and the emergent theme-store-like purveyors of vintage clothes.

British music critic Simon Reynolds coined the term 'retromania' for this obsession with an ever-more recent past, as everyone from pop stars to fashion designers dredges through recent decades for inspiration, be they purists who recreate a period look or the magpie who mixes different styles. He was writing in particular about pop culture and music but it applies to all aspects of society. Is the phenomenon a search for style – and even museification – in the absence of any dominant style or ideology today, where contemporary art, music and fashion are characterised by

their plurality (long hemlines or short? Oil painting, installation or video?) and there is the fabulous potential for picking and mixing the best from the past like a DJ? Are vintage addicts searching for lost glamour, or, as some have suggested, is it the 'kidults' phenomenon of not wanting to grow up and the reassurance of the Converse trainers, kitchen china and even school exercise books one had as a kid? Or, paradoxically, is it a search for the future, a nostalgia for the utopianism and optimism of the 50s and 60s? Somehow, nothing has ever seemed quite as 'modern' as the streamlined furniture, the bubble seats, blow-up chairs and plastic dresses of the 50s and 60s, or the silly haircuts and space shuttles of *Star Trek* and 70s sci-fi.

Secondhand also has its creative side: the inventiveness of assembling a retro look that, of course, doesn't really look at all like the past, or the recuperation, customising and recreation of handbags from leather jackets or new light fittings from old, allied to the ethos that secondhand shopping is not just money-saving but planet-saving, a green recyling movement, taking the used to come up with something new.

WHERE TO SHOP

EACH CHAPTER IN THIS BOOK HAS BEEN ARRANGED BY AREA, STARTING WITH THE FAMOUS RIGHT BANK (RIVE DROITE)/LEFT BANK (RIVE GAUCHE) DIVISION NORTH AND SOUTH OF THE RIVER SEINE, WITH ALL THE MYTHS THAT ARE ATTACHED (RIGHT BANK FOR BUSINESS AND COMMERCE, LEFT BANK OF INTELLECTUALS AND STUDENTS), AND THEN DIVIDED INTO THE DIFFERENT DISTRICTS THAT ARE OFTEN LIKENED TO A COLLECTION OF VILLAGES, EACH WITH ITS OWN DISTINCT STYLE – GEOGRAPHICAL, HISTORICAL AND SENTIMENTAL – AND THE CORRESPONDING STYLES OF SECONDHAND SHOPS.

The Marais has become a magnet for vintage clothes, St-Germain for designer furniture, although you may find more original stuff – and better bargains – in more offbeat districts like Montmartre, Pigalle, Oberkampf and the stalwarts of the Latin Quarter.

I have included opening hours, where possible, but purveyors of secondhand, vintage and junk are often one-man or one-woman shows, subject to whims, to closing up shop for a few hours or few days, as they attend a *braderie* (see the glossary on p11 for this and other French terms) or collect a chest of drawers, and many boutiques close for all or part of August.

Louvre/Les Halles
1st and 2nd arrondissements

Next to each other but almost diametrically opposed: the Louvre is the elegant planned Paris of grand squares, the Louvre and Palais-Royal palaces and some upmarket fashion surprises; Les Halles, the former wholesale market district, is dominated by the desultory Forum des Halles shopping centre, currently going through an attempt at re-redevelopment, though nonetheless the area contains some of Paris' best secondhand record shops and streetwise secondhand clothes. Further north are the *grands boulevards*, with their 19th century covered shopping arcades.

The Marais
3rd and 4th arrondissements

Famed for its stunning array of 17th and 18th century mansions, and the slightly unlikely combination of Paris' gay and Jewish districts, a cosmopolitan fashion hotspot, where you might well find more visitors than Parisians. There's a cluster of *friperies* and vintage clothing stores, while in the northern Marais contemporary art galleries are joined by modern design specialists.

Champs-Elysées/Passy
8th and 16th arrondissements

The hinterland of the celebrated avenue is business and smart residential, while smart Passy can prove surprisingly good hunting territory for lovers of upmarket fashion labels.

Montmartre/Pigalle/Batignolles
9th, 17th and 18th arrondissements

In the north of the city, Montmartre has a picturesque hill-village allure with cottages, artists' studios, windmills and even a vineyard, and keeps up its arty spirit with some unusual *brocantes*, as do neighbouring Batignolles and Pigalle, with their arty, creative populations and offbeat clothes and bric-a-brac.

Bastille/Oberkampf/Canal St-Martin
10th and 11th arrondissements

Revolutionary, *populaire* and multicultural but also the historic district of craft workshops and furniture makers, with specialists in *recup* (recuperation) and a young, tongue-in-cheek bunch of *brocantes* around rue du Marché Popincourt.

Latin Quarter
Mainly 5th arrondissement

The district of Roman remains and the medieval university quarter has a more boho spirit than neighbouring St-Germain, seen in quirky *brocantes*, specialists in historic costume and gas lamps, or an array of comic book sellers.

St-Germain-des-Prés/Montparnasse
6th arrondissement

The classic Paris of café society is literary, intellectual and classy, both for secondhand clothes and furniture, with galleries where industrial design has become a coveted art object.

GLOSSARY

The essential vocab for secondhand and vintage shopping in Paris.

Achât Purchase; if it's written on the shop hoarding, it means they buy objects as well as sell them.

Braderie A discount store, clearance sale or selling off cheaply.

Brocante Bric-a-brac shops and markets, used both for secondhand shops and for the antiques and collectors' fairs held around town, and their stallholders: the *brocanteurs*.

Chiner The art of hunting out, bargain hunting and unearthing secondhand treasures.

Débarras House clearance – or a junk room.

Dépôt-vente The equivalent of a consignment store, where people deposit goods – clothes or jewellery, furniture, etc – and where the proceeds of a sale are divided between the shop and the vendor; the price usually comes down after a few weeks if an item doesn't sell.

Fringues Slang for clothes.

Fripes Secondhand clothes, from *fripé*, as in crumpled or wrinkled; hence, *friperie*, a secondhand clothes shop.

Griffé Labelled, as in designer clothes and, hence, *dégriffé* when the label has been cut out.

Librairie Bookshop, not to be confused with library (*bibliothèque*).

Occasion Means secondhand, as in *livres d'occasion*, but sums up the optimistic mood of secondhand shopping, as *occasion* (event) can also imply opportunity.

Puces Paris' *marchés aux puces* or the flea markets, originally developed in the 19th century, when rag and bone men (*chiffonniers*) and scrap iron merchants (*ferrailleurs*) sold off their flea-ridden wares outside the city walls.

Salle de ventes Auction room.

Soldes Not 'sold' but the 'sales' – dates are set by the French state – lasting for six weeks from January to early February and mid-June to July. Essentially for new items, but some *brocantes* and secondhand stores join in the fun.

Stock Stock shops where fashion brands sell off the previous season's lines are sprinkled around town, but with particular concentrations (including Georges Rech, Sonia Rykiel) on rue d'Alésia in the 14th arrondissement and a more recent cluster of younger fashion labels (Maje, Les Petites) on rue de Marseille in the 10th.

Style As in 'style', but if something is in the *style de* a certain period, designer or artist, it means it's not actually of or by them but a later imitation or copy.

Troc Exchange or barter, although *c'est du troc* can also mean 'it's junk'. If you've got an item to get rid of, or you're looking to trade up in your collection, it can be worth trying. Look out also for *troc* parties (see p133), where objects are exchanged.

Vide grenier Literally an attic clearout: read the French equivalent of jumble sales or car boot sales, usually held out in the street by the residents of a particular neighbourhood.

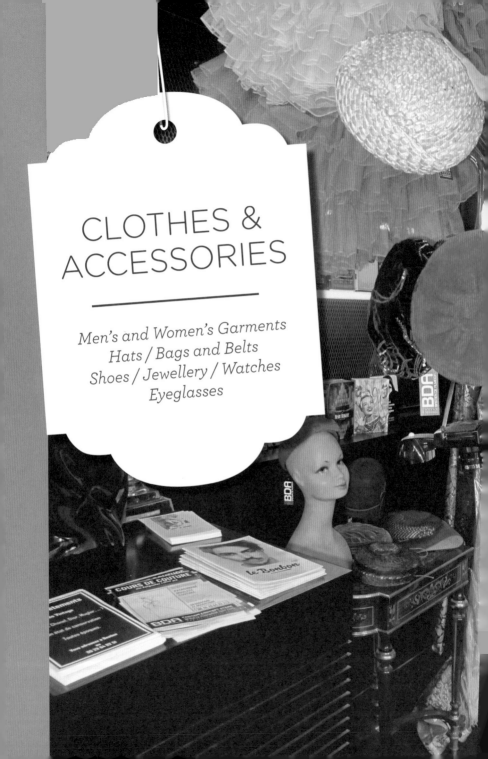

CLOTHES & ACCESSORIES

Men's and Women's Garments
Hats / Bags and Belts
Shoes / Jewellery / Watches
Eyeglasses

VINTAGE FASHION IN PARIS IS UNDERGOING AN INCREDIBLE TRANSFORMATION. TODAY, IT'S NO LONGER SIMPLY A QUESTION OF SECONDHAND AS AFFORDABLE, BUT OF SECONDHAND AS A WAY OF CREATING STYLE AND OF FINDING THE UNIQUE PIECE THAT NO ONE ELSE WILL BE WEARING.

On the shop front, secondhand clothes stores seem to split into two extremes: on the one hand, elegant boutiques with carefully sourced clothes and accessories, and bags that fetch four-figure sums, whether it's recent designer items or the true period vintage of hand-stitched, beaded or embroidered couture dresses that have perhaps marked fashion history; on the other, the cheap and cheerful, racks piled high with colourful cast-offs, and probably no design history at all.

Different districts reflect different styles. The 16th arrondissement consignment stores are reputed to be rich hunting grounds for upmarket cast-offs; St-Germain for jewellery and accessories. The Marais, apart from a few stand-out stores, seems to have been afflicted with identical stacks of Hawaiian shirts and flimsy dresses supplied in bulk that may be fun but are sometimes closer to fancy dress than dressing up. You can do better going to the shops where clothes are carefully selected, the better consignment stores, because at least these pieces come from individuals, the more original style mavens of Pigalle and Batignolles, the *brocantes* (secondhand markets) that pop up around town most weekends in summer or the specialists at the Puces de St-Ouen (see p110).

Legendary handbags like Hermès' Kelly or Chanel's quilted bags are highly sought after and expensive, but there are also fakes around. If you're prepared to fork out thousands, unless you're really certain of a bag's provenance buy from reputable specialists who are prepared to certify their pieces.

Some of the best shops are flamboyant like their owners – people who live, dress and think vintage. But while some secondhand style addicts go for the full-out retro look, legendary Parisian chic is more often about casual everyday vintage and the subtle art of accessorising: the Chanel jacket with jeans, or a great vintage handbag, the perfect shoes or *bijoux fantaisie* (costume jewellery) to provide the finishing touch to today's fashions.

Another trend is towards ecology and creative recycling, with jewellery made from old watches and artifacts by Delphine Pariente, handbags from used leather jackets at Matières à Réflexion or customised denim jackets at Célia Darling.

€€€
DIDIER LUDOT

20 and 24 Galerie de Montpensier, Jardins du Palais-Royal, 75001
01 42 96 06 56
www.didierludot.fr
Mon-Sat 10:30-19:00
Mᵒ Palais-Royal

Didier Ludot is the guru of vintage couture and his shops in the refined arcades of Palais-Royal are a very regal form of consignment store (yes, you can sell off family heirlooms and catwalk *cadeaux* here providing they make the cut). Goggle at the display cases – perhaps 1920s Jean Patou, a Lanvin evening gown from the 1930s, 70s Cardin and Dior, classic Givenchy and Balmain, or recent Jean-Paul Gaultier – to swot up on what to look for, even if you can't afford to buy it here. Ludot adheres to the vintage wine analogy with his belief that real vintage clothes must be a *grand cru*: hand-sewn and impeccably styled and cut. Two doors up, the accessories shop has collectors' must-have bags, and impressive jewellery, made for Balmain, Balenciaga, Chanel and others. On the other side of the gardens, it's Ludot's new dresses in La Petite Robe Noire inspired by Brigitte, Audrey *et al*.

€
ESPACE KILIWATCH

64 rue Tiquetonne, 75002
01 42 21 17 37
www.espacekiliwatch.fr
Mon 14:00-19:45; Tue-Sat 11:00-19:45
Mᵒ Etienne-Marcel

Espace Kiliwatch is a bit like the Tardis – the further you go inside, the more spaces open in front of you. There's some new (Levi's, Pepe, Soul Edge, Scotch & Soda), lots of old – clearly marked as 'Used' on the price tags – and a young clubby clientele that give this place a rave-era vibe, an impression kept up by the massive, though friendly, doorman. Some people criticise it for being a little pricey but it is more that prices vary a lot and, as the biggest vintage store in Paris, the sheer choice makes coming here worthwhile if you're after casual wear. Fortunately, despite the maze, sections are well organised, with a vast choice for both men and women, heavy on jeans and denim jackets. You'll also find reconditioned anoraks, retro-print shirts and summer dresses, a great stack of leather belts, and quirky bags.

€€

FORGET ME NOT

90 rue de Richelieu, 75002
09 82 39 10 19
Mon-Fri 10:30-19:00
M° Richelieu-Drouot or Bourse

Remember the days when handbags were handbags? Hafi Barron scouts out bags from all over Europe and even across the Atlantic, going for classic looks rather than legends (leather with gilt clasps and dainty handles, lots of neat crocodile numbers, some quirky 60s raffia), and then shows them off just as if they were today's fashion, behind a smart grey shopfront in a bright, well-lit boutique in the finance district near the Bourse.

€€

IGLAÏNE

12 rue de la Grande Truanderie, 75001
01 42 36 19 91
Mon-Sat 11:00-19:00
M° Etienne-Marcel/RER Châtelet-Les Halles

Iglaïne is a low-key favourite among Paris' vintage insiders, despite its unprepossessing location off seedy rue St-Denis, and eternally popular with film crews who pop in to borrow pieces for their shoots. With womenswear at the front, men's at the rear, the selection is high quality yet incredibly eclectic, ranging from theatrical beaded dresses and bouffant silks that you might just get away with at a Christmas party to some chic designer labels (Louis Féraud, Carven Couture, jackets by Christian Lacroix and Thierry Mugler) and dandy trousers, as well as some oddities like ethnic clothes from Mexico or the Sahara.

€€

LA MARELLE

25 Galerie Vivienne, 75002
01 42 60 08 19
www.galerie-vivienne.com
Mon-Fri 10:30-18:30; Sat 12:30-18:30
Mº Bourse or Palais-Royal

An upmarket *dépôt vente* in the grandest of Paris' beautiful 19th century covered shopping arcades, La Marelle is renowned for its good condition, up-to-date mid-range fashion labels, such as Gérard Darel, Chloé, Max Mara and Comme des Garçons, and a reputation for constantly changing stock. So, always worth keeping an eye on.

€€€

NEILA VINTAGE

28 rue du Mont-Thabor, 75001
01 42 96 88 70
Mon-Sat 10:30-19:00
Mº Tuileries

A small shop where vintage is all about exclusivity and luxury. Neila Jaziri seeks out pieces with a timeless quality that keeps them contemporary, so it's 60s to 90s established values (and valuable), like Yves Saint Laurent, Chanel and Givenchy, and a less-is-more philosophy, with just a fraction of the stock on show.

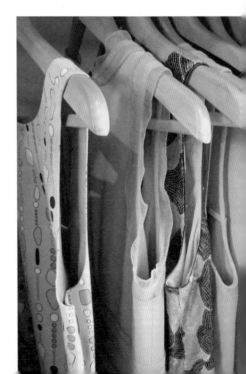

€€€

LES ANTIQUITÉS DE L'ILE SAINT-LOUIS

20 rue des Deux Ponts, 75004
01 43 29 27 77
www.isl-antiquites.com
Mon-Sat 11:00-19:00
M° Pont-Marie

Located just across from the Marais on the Ile St-Louis, Antiques at ISL really stands for designer accessories: Chanel and Hermès handbags and merchandising objects, Vuitton bags and luggage, Chanel and YSL costume jewellery and chain belts, sparklers from Bulgari and Van Cleef, and men's watches, which speaks a lot about vintage as investment. It's pricey, the display is uninspiring, and you have to buzz the door to get in, but there's lots of choice if you're after a rarer model, say a particular handbag, and items are certified as authentic. In the room behind, it's over to vintage furniture, mainly 1950s to 70s, such as Joe Colombo's fibreglass Elda chair, Pierre Paulin and Jacobsen chairs, Lurçat tapestries or a Mies van der Rohe Barcelona daybed.

€

BIS BOUTIQUE SOLIDAIRE

7 boulevard du Temple, 75003
01 44 78 11 08
www.bisboutiquesolidaire.fr
Tue-Sat 10:00-19:00
M° Filles du Calvaire or République

A charity shop with a touch of class. With its sleek black facade a few doors up from Merci (see p81) and brightly lit interior, nothing here cries out charity shop. Bis Boutique Solidaire gives new life to old clothes, stringently selected from the sacks of garments collected all over Paris by the Secours Catholique and doubling as a job creation scheme for the unemployed.

€

COIFFEUR VINTAGE

32 rue des Rosiers, 75004
01 40 27 04 98
Daily 11:00-21:00
M° St-Paul

A former Marais hairdressers turned vintage couture store (and a neat nod at the French dismissal of hairdressers' taste), this place has an almost cult following among the Marais *friperies*: small, crowded and very popular with young foreign tourists. At first glance it's hard to see why. The selection is definitely more *fripes* than true vintage, and much of it is run-of-the-mill, but if you dig deep into the tightly packed rails and quantities of 80s hippy-era crochet, *vichy* (gingham) blouses, fur coats and boots, you might just make a find.

€€

DELPHINE PARIENTE

8 rue de Turenne, 75004
01 42 71 84 64
www.delphinepariente.fr
Mon 15:00-19:00; Tue-Sat 11:00-19:00
(closed three weeks in Aug)
M° Bastille

Jewellery designer Delphine Pariente's most distinctive pieces use found objects in chain pendants combining old watches, bits of Victorian jewellery, coral beads, strass or a porcelain doll's arm. In her spacious new boutique she marries this recuperation aspect with her love for vintage furniture and vintage lighting, most of it for sale (though not the fabulous black metal petal light above the counter), staged like an apartment. There are also her delicate bracelets, engraved medallions and some vintage clothing, as well as a rail of previous season one-off Chloé samples.

€

FREE'P'STAR

8 rue Ste-Croix de la Bretonnerie, 75004
01 42 76 03 72
www.freepstar.com
Mon-Fri 11:00-21:00; Sat-Sun 12:00-21:00
M° Hôtel de Ville or St-Paul

Word play on *fripes*, French for
secondhand clothes, and free (well it's
not quite, but almost), Free 'P' Star has a
chaotic array of clothes hung on racks and
stuffed in cardboard boxes, often at much
lower prices than you'll find elsewhere, if
you know what you're looking for. It tends
to get very crowded as the dedicated trawl
through checked shirts, lurid prints and
army jackets, as well as the bins of odds
and ends for a euro. You might just pick
up some genuine vintage bags and skirts,
or funky hats.

Other locations
61 rue de la Verrerie, 75004
20 rue de Rivoli, 75004

€

FRIP'IRIUM

2 rue de la Verrerie, 75004
01 40 29 95 57
Tue-Sat 13:00-21:00; Sun 14:00-21:00
M° Hôtel de Ville or St-Paul

With that inimitable, slightly musty
smell of old clothing, it's A-line skirts
for her, Hawaiian shirts for him, some
wild-looking thigh boots, and a cellar of
cast-offs for only five euros. Everything is
so crammed in here, you can barely make
your way past the rails, especially when
there are a few other people in the shop.

€

HIPPY MARKET LE TEMPLE

21 rue du Temple, 75004
09 62 24 69 09
www.hippy-market.fr
Mon-Sat 11:00-20:00; Sun 14:00-20:00
M° Hôtel de Ville

One of a growing number of Hippy
Market stores in France, supplied by the
massive Eureka enterprise in Rouen,
which delivers lorry loads of secondhand
clothes all over Europe, this is a shop
pushing its green credentials: be happy,
be green, recycle, re-wear... And although
the flowers painted on the plate-glass
storefront are a little off-putting, once
inside it's a pleasant surprise: cheerful
and unpretentious, with rails of clothing,
apparently mainly sorted by colour.
There are denim jackets in blue, yellow
or orange, bright shirts, retro dresses,
some real croco handbags, and a cheerful
Woodstock vibe of pumping 70s rock,
orange and apple ice boxes, vintage
thermoses and old LPs.

€

KING OF THE FRIP

33 rue du Roi de Sicile, 75004
01 42 78 33 72
Mon-Sat 11:00-19:30
M° St-Paul

For those with an unrequited love of
Hawaiian shirts, the 'king of secondhand
clothes' adheres to the pile-it-in ethos,
keeping this place busy with young
hopefuls as they rummage among racks
laden with loud print dresses, short-sleeve
shirts, army surplus and denim jackets,
and a stack of homburg hats that could
either be this year's trend or last year's
cast-offs. There's a lot of trash, still it has a
little more space than some of its Marais
rivals, and even a decent changing room.

MARAIS BITES

At Jaja you can expect plenty of good wines, many of them organic

JAJA

3 rue Sainte-Croix de la Bretonnerie, 75004
01 42 74 71 52
www.jaja-resto.com

Well placed for all the Marais vintage *friperies*, Jaja takes its name from a casual term for 'plonk', so you can expect plenty of good wines, many of them organic, as well as satisfying bistro food – heirloom tomatoes, good steaks – in a pleasant loft-like space with vintage lights and chairs, hidden in a courtyard. Open lunch and dinner, with good value formules for lunch.

CAFÉ CHARLOT

38 rue de Bretagne, 75003
01 44 54 03 30
www.cafecharlotparis.com

A converted belle époque bakery, refurbished in 50s style with zinc bar and globe lights, has become a fashionable hotspot where the Marais gay, fashion and art sets all converge. A good place for a casual drink, classic croques, steak tartare and bistro dishes or Sunday brunch, but above all a rendezvous for observing the scene from its corner terrace.

€€

MADE IN USED

36 rue de Poitou, 75003
01 42 76 98 21
www.madeinused.com
Tue-Sat 11:00-19:30 (closed 14:00-14:30);
Sun 13:30-19:00
M° Filles du Calvaire

Up in the hip Haut (Northern) Marais, Italian fashion consultant Vic Caserta mysteriously describes his collection of 40s to 90s clothing as "genetic vintage" and it's possibly just an excuse for high prices, with a starchy shop assistant to match. Sift well: there are some stylish 50s dresses and crochet bags, but some of the more unremarkable pieces, such as denim jackets, are outrageously expensive.

€€

MATIÈRES À RÉFLEXION

19 rue de Poitou, 75003
01 42 72 16 31
www.matieresareflexion.com
Mon-Sat 12:00-19:00; Sun 15:00-19:00
M° Filles du Calvaire

Up in the Haut Marais fashion heartland, vintage meets ecology at Matières à Réflexion, which cleverly recycles vintage leather jackets into soft new leather bags, handmade in its Paris workshop and sold alongside a laidback selection of casual clothes and jewellery. There are various models but all are just a little bit different depending on the original jacket: tones of black or brown, the patina of usage, surviving seams, little zips, and even useful pockets. The leather is super soft and lined with cotton. Bags can also be made to order from your own much-loved leather jacket or one chosen from their stock (count three to four weeks for fabrication).

MAM'ZELLE SWING

€€

35 bis rue du Roi de Sicile, 75004
01 48 87 04 06
www.mamzelleswing.fr
Mon-Sat 14:00-19:00
M° Hôtel de Ville

Just when the endless flotsam among the cluster of rather similar *friperies* in this part of the Marais is beginning to get you down, along comes Mam'zelle Swing. Mam'zelle Swing (Berenice) herself is there in person, dressed in vintage at her 50s counter, with swing and bebop wafting in the background and enticing window displays. It's womenswear only, from 1900 to the 60s, with a 40s and 50s bias – although there is also some earlier stuff, and I've also spotted a 60s scarlet Courrèges mini coat. She clearly loves seeking out her well selected, ironed and repaired pieces, with everything well labelled and clearly priced, and prime pieces displayed on wooden mannequins: waisted New Look dresses, girlie collars, some good handbags, dainty hats, winged

This is a great place if you're looking for a real dress with a period feel, something for a party or a Bakelite brooch

sunglasses and costume jewellery too. This is a great place if you're looking for a real dress with a period feel, something for a party or a Bakelite brooch, and although the shop is small, for once there's enough space to actually look and appreciate what there is.

€€

LE MONDE SECRET

21 rue St-Paul, 75004
01 42 74 47 21
Thu-Sat 14:30-18:30
M° St-Paul or Sully Morland

At her small shop in the St-Paul enclave, Anne Desbrueres has a fabulous selection of classic Bakelite or silver art deco jewellery, as well as mirrors and moulded glass art deco lamps.

€€

ODETTA VINTAGE

76 rue des Tournelles, 75003
01 48 87 28 61,
www.odettavintage.com
Tue-Sat 14:00-19:30; Sun 15:00-19:00
M° Chemin-Vert

The duo of Valérie Nizan and Charles Estevez mix secondhand fashion and vintage furniture, so you might find Eames, Jacobsen or Saarinen chairs, and a lot of funky 60s lights, displayed rather as if it were a gallery, alongside necklaces and bags. Clotheswise, they "put the emphasis on the wearable," which means mainly recent tops and dresses, and some vintage evening wear. They complement glamorous shoes, perhaps by Alaia or Sergio Rossi, with their own range of new ankle boots and sandals.

€€
LE VINTAGE BAR

16 rue de la Verrerie, 75004
01 42 74 56 95,
Mon-Sat 11:00-20:00; Sun 13:00-20:00
M° Hôtel de Ville or St-Paul

On the street that has become the focus of secondhand shopping in the Marais, the Vintage Bar is for lovers of glitz and colour. Think colour-shock shoes (platforms, baby doll stilettos), diamanté glasses, inexpensive sparkly rings and trinkets. Pricier and more upmarket than the other secondhand stores on this stretch, Le Vintage Bar stocks a few labels; perhaps YSL shoes, a Chanel bag, a Cacharel jacket or Paco Rabanne. A spiral staircase plastered with Marilyn photos leads to a cellar of discount evening wear that goes from lovely to horrendous.

€€
STUDIO W

6 rue du Pont-aux-Choux, 75003
01 44 78 05 02
Tue-Sun 14:00-19:30
M° St-Sébastien-Froissart

Studio W is an insider haunt of fashion stylists, loved for its individually chosen pieces from the 1920s on, and the charm and discerning taste of owner William Moricet. He's happy to talk you through his different pieces, although it's the accessories – shoes, handbags and costume jewellery, ranging from fine art deco to 70s catwalk show-stoppers – that are often more interesting than the clothes. Not all the jewellery is on display; ask and he can bring more pieces out of his stock.

€€

VIOLETTE ET LÉONIE

**27 rue de Poitou and 1 rue de Saintonge,
75003
01 44 59 87 35
www.violetteleonie.com
Mon 13:00-19:30; Tue-Sat 11:00-19:30;
Sun 14:00-19:00
Mᵒ Fille du Calvaire**

The discrete grey minimalist facade
quietly says 'Marais fashion' rather than
screams out 'secondhand', for Violette
et Léonie prides itself on being a *dépôt
vente concept* rather than a mere *dépôt
vente*: they insist on recent clothes in
perfect condition, with a rapid turnover to
keep pieces current and seasonal. Items
remain on sale for two months before
they have to be collected or are given to
charity. Clothes range from high street
to high end and there can be some good
finds from today's rising labels, such as
Maje, although when it comes to H&M and
Zara, you probably might just as well go to
H&M and Zara and buy the items new.

€€€

DÉPÔT VENTE DE PASSY

**14 rue de la Tour, 75116
01 45 20 95 21
www.depot-vente-luxe.fr
Tue-Sat 10:30-19:00
Mᵒ Passy**

Paris' consignment stores resemble the
residents of its different districts and
here in upmarket, conservative Passy,
it's upmarket clothes from ladies who've
practically never worn them, with rails of
Prada and Chanel. Prices are high, sizes
mainly small. There's also menswear and
children's clothes.

Other location
Dépôt vente du 17e, 109 rue de
Courcelles, 75017.

€€€

RÉCIPROQUE

89, 92, 93, 95, 97, 101 rue de la Pompe, 75016
01 47 04 30 28
www.reciproque.fr
Tue-Fri 11:00-19:00; Sat 10:30-19:00
M° Rue de la Pompe

Réciproque claims to be the largest *dépôt vente* in Paris, going strong since 1978. In fact it operates six side-by-side boutiques and, given its smart 16th arrondissement location, the emphasis is on upmarket classics, staid but sure. At 93-95, it's designer labels, with daywear one side, evening wear the other. Everything is neatly pressed and hung on rails, organised by style, brand or size, in something of the atmosphere of a dry cleaners. It's the place to find a classic Chanel jacket, a barely touched Givenchy suit and smart blouses that look like new. For the evening, there might be flashier Gaultier and Dolce & Gabbana, a long Dior silk sheath or vibrant Valentino. Shoes and less-elitist clothes are crammed into the basement. Two doors up, it's rails of bags, scarves and a basement of raincoats. Curiously, accessories are not Réciproque's strong point: 16th arrondissement ladies hold on to their classic, timeless bags and get rid of more transient clothes.

€€

THE DATE

3 rue de la Tour, 75116
09 52 35 18 39
Tue-Sat 11:00-19:00 (closed 14:00-15:00)
M° Passy

"I like things that have a soul," says Isabelle, who opened this refreshing new *dépôt vente* in spring 2012, and she's proud to be very selective: "I take things that are amusing, chic; if it's banal I don't take it." She looks out for fine materials, a good cut and unusual pieces, so that the choice is small but pertinent. There's some vintage, more recent stuff, mixing top-end labels and funkier pieces, a small selection of new scarves, bags and jewellery, and a window display that catches the eye.

€€

LA BOUTIQUE NOIRE

22 rue La Vieuville, 75018
09 53 20 46 17
Tue-Fri/Sun 14:00-19:30; Sat 11:30-19:30
M° Abbesses

With a black shopfront and only a discrete *'dépôt'* and *'achat'* painted on the window, the 'Black Boutique' is not for those trying to be retro but for up-to-date clothes that don't look secondhand. Here it's a younger, trendier selection than the traditional Chanel brigade, going from Top Shop tops to Jean-Paul Gaultier, Chloé, Claudie Pierlot and Acne jeans and a high chance of finding a good condition leather jacket.

€

CHINE MACHINE

100 rue des Martyrs, 75018
01 80 50 27 68
www.chinemachinevintage.com
Daily 12:00-20:00
M° Abbesses

Behind its new agey mantra of "rambling rummagers sifting through the accumulation of the ages" lies an apparently unsorted jumble with a hippy edge, strong on long brocade dresses and snazzy sunglasses. This Montmartre shop has its ups and downs, but it's the sort of place where you can make occasional finds, perhaps killer heels or a Hermès scarf, in a spirit of exchange and *troc*. During the week bring in your own items for cash or exchange, or as they put it on their blog: "Liberate your unworn clothes from the prison of the back of your closet."

CÉLIA DARLING

a good mix of chic and casual: slinky party tops, chunky jumpers, a rail of designer labels

€ €

5 rue Henri Monnier, 75009
01 56 92 19 12
Mon-Sat 12:30-20:00
M° St-Georges or Pigalle

Célia ("Darling is not my real name") is an inveterate *chiner*, searching out vintage clothes from Brick Lane (London) and Brussels as well as Paris and combining it all with a bright tongue-in-cheek retro setting – old radio cabinets, lamps, coat stands, fairground animal masks on the shop mannequins and dainty new hats created by her friend Carlotta Laurier. The feel is young and contemporary, rather than secondhand, with a good mix of chic and casual: slinky party tops, chunky jumpers, a rail of designer labels, such as Yves Saint Laurent, Guy Laroche and Louis Féraud, and funky customised vintage pieces that Célia rustles up in the workshop at the rear. Creating new from old, she might adorn denim shorts with a cowrie-shell trim, touch-up 60s dresses or crop a wasp-waisted vintage dress into a bustier, and has developed a neat line in denim jackets adorned with tiger's head medallions made from African fabrics and cross-stitch dogs cut out of old tapestry pictures.

BDA
BASTIEN
DE ALMEIDA

€€

46 rue La Condamine, 75017
01 42 93 54 70
www.bastiendealmeida.com
Tue-Sat 11:00-20:00
M° Place de Clichy or La Fourche

Up on the arty, boho street in Les
Batignolles where Renoir once had
a studio, the black walls and silver
mannequins at BDA Bastien de Almeida
create a 70s disco feel for the shop's
flamboyant selection of vintage party
dresses and evening wear. Hats sit on a
line of glass and china heads; a curious
ostrich emerges from the wall; there
are fashion books and DVDs of cult
fashionista movies and musicals (Esther
Williams, Dietrich), with *Ziegfeld Follies*
playing on a video screen on my last visit.

"I became passionate about vintage," says Almeida, who sports a casual dandy look (pencil moustache, vintage trousers), "because I loved Hollywood cinema of the 1940s and 50s, so I loved the actresses and the clothes they wore." For him, vintage can mean anything from the 1920s to 80s, it's not the label that counts but the style, and what is essential is "clothes that represent a period." His customers are in search of clothes that are unique and a glamour that no longer exists, although as he admits, the sort of dresses that used to be daywear are now things you wear in the evening. "At the beginning I bought a lot in San Francisco and LA, it was all American. Now it is vintage labels and mainly French." That means Guy Laroche, Yves Saint Laurent, unnamed glories, lace dresses, Versace, lots of red and orange and some braided jackets that could come straight out of *Sergeant Pepper*.

Most dresses are reasonably priced and, except for truly exceptional ones, come in the €100-€150 range. Almeida began as a fashion stylist and he also makes clothes to measure, runs in-house couture lessons, and can adapt his vintage finds to fit. If you try something on you'll be let into the downstairs cellar boudoir. Almeida's favourite labels? No hesitation: "My fetish designer Yves Saint Laurent, and Jean-Louis Scherrer of the 70s and 80s."

"I became passionate about vintage because I loved Hollywood cinema"

BASTIEN DE ALMEIDA

€

FRIPES KETCHUP

8 rue Dancourt, 75018
01 42 51 96 33
www.fripesketchup.com
Mon-Fri/Sun 14:00-20:00; Sat 11:00-20:00
(closed 13:00-14:00)
M° Abbesses or Anvers

Getting away from cacophonous crates of clothes or retro as nostalgia, Fripes Ketchup is about the art of staying in the sauce and cleverly helping you sort through the jungle. Here secondhand clothes from the 50s to 90s from all over France are astuciously assembled into complete looks that suit today's trends and are displayed on hangers in an industrial loft-style setting.

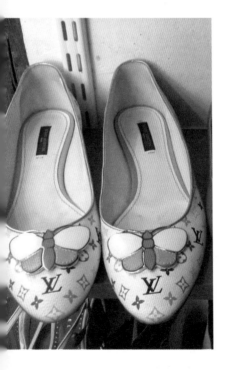

€

GUERRISOL

19 avenue de Clichy, 75017
01 40 08 03 00
www.guerrisol.com
Mon-Sat 10:00-19:30
M° Place de Clichy

A legendary address where secondhand really does means cheap (and none-too-clean). Don't believe it when they say this place is popular with fashionistas – it's mainly frequented by the population of Paris' poorer districts – but if you have the courage and the time to rummage, then there are simply thousands of (sometimes very) used clothes and shoes. Only for the brave.

Other locations
17bis boulevard de Rochechouart, 75009
45 boulevard de la Chapelle, 75018

€€

ZACH & SAM

13 rue Clauzel, 75009
01 42 81 47 82
Tue-Sat 10:30-19:30 (closed August)
M° St-Georges

A rare *dépôt vente* that's just for men, which adheres to its "cool but chic" maxim, with laidback background music and neatly sorted belts, sunglasses, casual wear and suits in good condition.

MONTMARTRE BITES

fresh seasonal cuisine served in a vintage bistro setting

MIROIR

94 rue des Martyrs, 75018
01 46 06 50 73

One of the young new bistronomiques that have recently reached Montmartre, with fresh seasonal cuisine served in a vintage bistro setting, and a wine shop across the street.

HÔTEL AMOUR

8 rue Navarin, 75009
01 48 78 31 80
www.hotelamourparis.fr

This hip yet relaxed fashion hangout inside the arty cool Hôtel Amour is great if you're doing Pigalle's vintage boutiques and *brocantes*. The ground floor bar-bistro is 70s retro, and there are also plenty of tables outside in the overgrown courtyard. All day service and a menu of old-fashioned favourites from radishes to roast chicken or fish and chips.

€€

69 rue de Rochechouart, 75009
01 42 81 10 42
www.mamie-vintage.com
Mon 14:30-19:30; Tue-Sat 11:30-19:30
(closed 13:30-14:30)
M° Anvers

As soon as you go into the boutique you know you've found a treasure trove, piled high with waisted New Look dresses, astonishing hats and diamanté brooches, clutch bags and sunglasses, men's dandy suits, caps, blousons and a window full of two-tone shoes, all watched over by Mamie, alias Brigitte, in love-curled hair, pencilled eyebrows and retro pedal pushers, and her colleague Yannick. They also do great re-edited pearly bags, make their own small line of neo-50s floral summer dresses, hire out clothes and can copy vintage clothes in your size.

"It all comes from rock and roll," says Brigitte, whose past at some point included studies at Sciences Po (Paris Institute of Political Sciences) and a doctorate in law before she saw the error of her ways and devoted herself to a love of rock and roll, 78s and the whole lifestyle that goes with it. "I started collecting because I was looking for 40s-style trousers and couldn't find them," she says. She opened the shop in 1992 and was one of the movers behind the revival of the *guinguette* dance halls along the River Marne with the Guinguette du Martin-Pêcheur and its Miss Guinguette competition.

Pleased that more and more young people are also interested in vintage, Brigitte also runs a 'relooking' service that can kit you out with the complete retro outfit, hair, make-up and petticoats, whether it's for going out to a party or a sober yet curvaceous day at the office.

MAMIE BLUE VINTAGE SPIRIT

€€

CHEZ CHIFFONS

47 rue de Lancry, 75010
06 64 26 11 98,
www.chezchiffons.fr
Tue-Fri 11:00-19:00; Sat 13:00-19:00
M° République or Jacques-Bonsergent

Doris Homburg used to be a dresser for the cinema, so it's not surprising that the window display of her tiny shop near the Canal St-Martin resembles a miniature film set: a waisted floral New Look dress on one side and a birdcage containing a Jacques Fath shoe on the other hint at the style to come. Inside, it's a stringently directed selection for those after a feminine period look, with a global mix of designer labels (lots of French and US) and the anonymous. It's particularly good for 50s bustier dresses for setting off your curves, though you might also find a transparent 30s voile number, an 80s Ungaro print or recent Michael Perry shoes. She also runs an occasional vintage stall on Sunday at Brunch Bazaar at Wanderlust (see p133), the rooftop restaurant of the Cité de la Mode fashion and design centre.

€€

COME ON EILEEN

16 rue des Taillandiers, 75011
01 43 38 12 11
Mon-Fri 11:00-20:00; Sat 14:00-20:00
M° Bastille or Ledru-Rollin

Named after the Dexys Midnight Runners hit, even the neon lettering on the facade has a timewarp feel at this Bastille vintage store committed to the colourful 70s and 80s, and memories of the days of flares, big lapels, floppy hats and shaggy coats. With men's and women's wear and even some clothes for kids, it's designer-led and pricey on the ground floor, and cheerful and more affordable in the huge basement, which is stacked up high with clutter, from glitzy tops to jeans and Converse trainers, and handbags dangling from the ceiling.

Other location
40 rue de Rivoli, 75004

€€

LA MODE VINTAGE

12 rue Rochebrune, 75011
06 63 79 72 04
www.la-mode-vintage.com
Fri/Sat 11:00-19:00; or by appointment
Mᵒ Voltaire

Effortlessly at ease in her 1970s Yves Saint Laurent, former fashion stylist Carol Biegelman began with a stall at the flea market before opening her shop, and is also a stalwart of the Salon du Vintage (see p135) and Puces de Design (see p134). Her classy selection shows a distinct predilection for the 70s of the aforementioned Yves Saint Laurent, as well as Lanvin and the graphic prints of Leonard – it helps if you like flashy colours – although there's also plenty of 90s and later. Great bags too.

€

DÉBUT

28 avenue Laumière, 75019
01 40 18 02 74
Tue-Thu 10:00-19:30 (closed 13:00-14:00);
Fri 12:00-20:00; Sat 10:00-19:30 (closed
13:00-14:30)
Mᵒ Lumière

Slightly out of Paris' main shopping districts on an avenue leading up to the Parc des Buttes-Chaumont, Début mixes secondhand clothes with costume jewellery and a rail of quirky clothing from young designers. I've seen some good finds here, wearable clothes from brands like Jil Sander, Thierry Mugler, Gérard Darel and Georges Rech, and shoes from Sonia Rykiel and Manolo Blahnik. There's also a decent size changing room. And if you want to know what the future has in store, the owner also does tarot and Yi-king by appointment.

OMAYA VINTAGE

29 rue Jean-Pierre-Timbaud, 75011
01 42 01 77 31
www.omaya-vintage.com
Mon-Sat 10:00-19:30
M° Oberkampf or République

Friendly staff, a thumping rock beat, an old guitar, keyboards and an ancient manual typewriter set the scene for men's and women's clothing with a 70s and 80s bias. There are Burberry and Pendleton jackets, some vintage dresses, streetwise Doc Martens and a stack of 80s sunglasses all at ten euros a pair. If at first sight it looks quite run-of-the-mill, the selection turns out to be particularly good for leather or denim jackets, authentic American baseball jackets, and even an unusual sportswear section – this is the only place where I've come across cycling jerseys, covered in vibrant sponsors' logos; just perfect for satisfying your Tour de France ambitions.

OPTIQUE DURABLE

2 rue Amelot, 75011
01 48 06 38 50
www.optiquedurable.fr
Tue-Sat 10:30-19:00 (closed 13:00-14:30)
M° Bastille

Taking the line that recycling is ecological, optician David Benhaim opened his own optician totally dedicated to vintage glasses frames; vintage but never used, bought up from old factory stocks and opticians' store cupboards, most of them manufactured in the Jura in France and in countless styles, be they square from the 40s or *Star Trek* from the 70s. Keeping up the spirit, the shop fittings came from an optician in the south of France, along with items found at the *puces* – but the lenses themselves are new and high quality, cut and fitted on the spot, and all frames can be adapted for your vision or for use as sunglasses.

THANX GOD I'M A VIP

€ - €€€

12 rue de Lancry, 75010
01 42 03 02 09
www.thanxgod.com
Tue-Sat 14:00-20:00
M° République

Thanx God for Sylvie Chateigner, one of the movers of the Paris club scene in the 1990s, who has moved address but keeps up her astute eclectic touch, with classy 60s and 70s clothing, stringently arranged by colour and keeping up with the seasons. "I spend a lot of time explaining to the French what vintage is. It's like wine, a good bottle will get better with age, but a tacky acrylic jumper will always be a tacky acrylic jumper," she says.

"It's like wine, a good bottle will get better with age, but a tacky acrylic jumper will always be a tacky acrylic jumper"

Sylvie Chateigner

In fact, part of the skill of running a vintage store, she says, "is always keeping it restocked," especially as the many fashion designers among her customers have a tendency to come here and buy in bulk, whether they're acquiring pieces for their personal collections or seeking inspiration in a vintage collar or a particular cut of sleeve. "My real job is an unearther of pieces," she says, and Sylvie has a great nose for seeking out supplies – on one occasion, a warehouse full of never-worn 70s Yves Saint Laurent and other designers' end of season stock; more recently, "after two trips to Italy and lots of negotiation," a stock of pristine, still unwrapped Aquascutum and Burberry tweed coats from the 60s and 70s ("better than those made today") from a shop that had closed in Italy.

Prices are high, but Sylvie is keen to keep the social mix that made her club nights stand out – "I want the young to come here too" – so she's opened a basement where everything is priced between €5 and €50, keeping up the concern for vintage style, though without the famous names.

€

GÉNÉRIQUE

68 rue du Cardinal Lemoine, 75005
01 46 34 04 23
Mon 15:00-19:30; Tue-Sat 11:00-19.30
(closed 13:00-15:00)
M° Cardinal-Lemoine

This tiny shocking-pink shop has plenty of local aficionados and is the sort of small low-key *dépôt vente* where you can make some good finds, its racks tightly packed with wearable women's clothes for low prices and a window awash with costume jewellery.

€€

LES MAUVAIS GARÇONS

10 rue de l'Arbalète, 75005
01 46 34 44 44
www.les-mauvais-garcons-depotvente.com
Tue-Fri 12:00-19:30; Sat 10:00-19:30
M° Censier-Daubenton

This ancient stone building used to be a notorious 'exchangist' club. Now it's dedicated to a different sort of exchange as a *dépôt vente*, with friendly staff and well-selected and organised stock. The focus is on recent designer labels, whether it's Chanel or Dolce & Gabbana, with shelves of bags, a whole wall of shoes and consignment goods supplemented by end of series items and last season's stock.

€

MICHEL WEBER ANTIQUITÉS BROCANTE

6 rue de l'Arbalète, 75005
01 43 31 64 91
www.weber-antiquites.com
Thu/Sat 11:00-19:00

At his intriguing little shop near the rue Mouffetard food market, Michel Weber lovingly puts together a display of real antique costumes and *objets de virtu*. Mother-of-pearl opera glasses, delicate hand-painted fans, carved walking sticks, a beaded cape, embroidered waistcoats, a pile of top hats, an impossibly wasp-waisted 1890s robe, beaded bags and purses, glass flacons for smelling salts or a 1920s leather cigar case – all evoke the elegance of times past. Weber is passionate and knowledgeable about his finds, and if some pieces are for serious collectors and historians, others are still useable today, attracting casual passers-by looking to accessorise an outfit, designers in search of inspiration, or the members of Carnet de Bals, an association that dresses up in period costume and reenacts 19th century balls in country châteaux.

€€€

ADRENALINE

30 rue Racine, 75006
01 44 27 09 05
www.adrenaline-vintage.com
Mon-Sat 11:00-19:00 (closed Aug)
M° Odéon or RER Luxembourg

A sleek, chic address near the Odéon theatre, where the speciality is vintage luggage and handbags, including classic Vuitton monogrammed suitcases and Hermès for hefty prices. Jewellery, watches, shoes, hats and a few clothes complete the look.

€€

ALEXANDRA ZEANA

19 rue de l'Echaudé, 75006
01 46 33 68 92/06 80 38 36 78
www.alexandrazeana.com
Mon-Sat 09:00-18:00 (closed 12:00-14:00)
M° Mabillon or St-Germain-des-Prés

Zeana has a magpie eye and a taste for fine workmanship and she loves showing off her discoveries. A mix of one-off pieces made by independent designers and a personal selection of antique and vintage jewellery, art deco bracelets and brooches, and raw amber or coral necklaces are displayed in a tiny boudoir-like boutique amid evening bags, antique chairs, crystal wine glasses and other objects.

DÉPÔT VENTE DE BUCI BOURBON

€€€

4 rue du Buci-Bourbon, 75006
01 46 34 28 28
Tue-Sat 11:00-19:00
Mᵒ Mabillon

A longstanding St-Germain consignment store, where the offhand staff are not much help but leave you free to browse through racks that are deep in designer labels – Yves Saint Laurent, Scherrer, Lanvin, etc. – crocodile bags, and plenty of shoes. Don't come here for the latest stuff to come off the catwalks, but for good-quality classics.

CHERCHEMINIPPES

€

102 (women), 109 (home and interiors), 110 (baby and children), 111 (men), 114 (haute couture and Japanese designers) and 124 (accessories) rue du Cherche-Midi, 75006
01 45 44 97 96
www.chercheminippes.com
Mon-Sat 11:00-19:00 (closed mid-July to mid-Aug)
Mᵒ Duroc or Falguière

This series of *dépôt ventes* on rue du Cherche Midi was a pioneer among secondhand stores in Paris and although the storefront has remained firmly in the 70s, the interior of the spacious women's shop at No.102 is a good source for recent fashion. For once the clothes are well sorted, either by label for current in-brands like See by Chloé, Vanessa Bruno, Sandro, Tara Jarman or Isabel Marant, or by size for more miscellaneous trousers, skirts and dresses. A well-controlled turnover keeps things seasonal and, despite a grouchy reputation, the atmosphere is busy and cheerful. The kids' store is also well worth a look for a big choice of baby and children's wear, baby equipment, children's books and toys.

DOURSOUX

€€

3 passage Alexandre, 75015
01 43 27 00 97
www.doursoux.com
Tue-Sat 10:00-19:30
Mᵒ Montparnasse-Bienvenüe or Pasteur

Poised in a shack next to a bit of flyover in redeveloped Montparnasse, Doursoux is a military surplus institution. There's a huge stock of clothing from combat trousers and army shirts to Foreign Legion kepis, some vintage, some reedited, with high prices for authentic Second World War garb. There's equipment too, including stretchers, tents and sleeping bags.

€€

L'EMBELLIE

2 rue du Regard, 75006
01 45 48 29 82
Tue-Sat 11:00-19:00
M° Sèvres-Babylone

Hidden on a side street opposite a fine *hôtel particulier* (grand townhouse), L'Embellie is a place that restores your faith in *dépôt ventes* and the image of Parisian chic, with upmarket labels and nothing but, both for smart evenings out and everyday wear. Everything here is on consignment from the local ladies who lunch, with elegant labels like Paule Ka, Sonia Rykiel, Chloé, agnès b, Armano Vintilo, Valentino and Hermès. An array of desirable shoes might include Louis Vuitton pumps, YSL heels and some extraordinary Walter Steiger patent platforms.

Other location
45 av de la Bourdonnais, 75007

€€

LES GINETTES

4 rue de Sabot, 75006
01 42 22 45 14
www.lesginettes.net
Tue-Sat 11:00-19:00 (closed Aug)
M° Mabillon

Up-to-date brands like Zadig et Voltaire and Isabel Marant are the focus at this *dépôt vente*, with good condition clothes displayed amid changing art and photo shows in an ancient, warped building in St-Germain, along with a few vintage pieces and eclectic china and household objects. The mood is friendly and casual and on Saturdays they offer mint tea.

€€€

KARRY'O

62 rue des Saints-Pères, 75007
01 45 48 94 67
www.karryo.com
Mon-Sat 10:30-19:00
M° St-Germain-des-Prés

The small pearl-grey boutique is elegant
like the district, with a glittery chandelier
and jewellery displayed amid sculptures.
Karry, alias Karine Berrebi, showcases
her own 70s-inspired designs in gold,
silver plate and semi-precious stones
alongside vintage items. She has a taste
for big necklaces and long chains, or the
extravagant parures designed by Roger
Scémama for couturiers like Lanvin and
Yves Saint Laurent, and precious ladies'
bracelet watches by Cartier, Jaeger Le
Coultre and Van Cleef & Arpels. Nothing
here has a price tag (think high).

€

MADAME DE...

65 rue Daguerre, 75014
01 77 10 59 46
www.madamede.net
Tue-Sat 11:00-19:30; some Sun mornings
(closed mid-July to mid-Aug)
M° Denfert-Rochereau or Gaîté

Named after the book by Louise de
Vilmorin and the 1953 Max Ophuls
film, about a pair of earrings endlessly
changing hands, Madame de... *'dépôt
vente retro et contemporain'* gets away
from the usual consignment store clutter.
The owner is selective, prices are fair and,
while it's mainly recent women's clothes
in good condition, the pieces that change
hands here include a small but authentic
selection of vintage, such as fabulous
60s orange mini-dresses, to attract real
vintage fans. Eclectic household china
and knick-knacks help to keep up the
retro edge.

Les Trois Marches de Catherine B

€€€

1 and 3 rue Guisarde, 75006
01 43 54 74 18
www.catherine-b.com
Mon-Sat 10:30-19:30
M° Mabillon

It's vintage Hermès and Chanel and nothing else from Catherine B, who began as a collector before deciding to share her passion in a minuscule boutique behind the Marché St-Germain almost 20 years ago. She explains how the shop was born: "A small ten metre square boutique to start off and be sure to only sell beautiful items." Expansion came next, pushing the boutique out into the shop next door.

As well as selling, Catherine B continues to collect clothes and accessories for herself: "The piece that I'm proudest of is the very first Birkin bag made by Hermès in 1984 and created for Jane Birkin." She bought the bag at auction in 2000 and occasionally puts it on show.

If you're after a particular period piece, she has all sorts of variants on the classic Chanel tweed jacket, Chanel quilted bags, big pearl and chain necklaces, and baubles galore. There are Hermès silk scarves, boldly printed silk dresses and the Birkin and Kelly bags that sometimes reach five-figure sums, as well as a few more debateable items, like Chanel snow boots, probably best classified as curios.

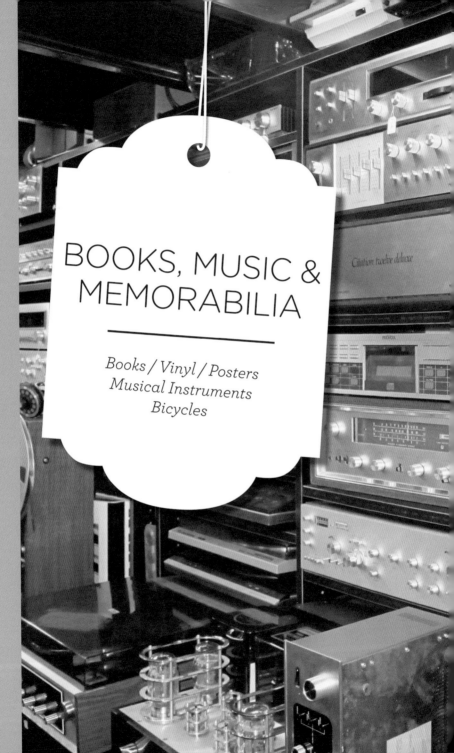

BOOKS, MUSIC & MEMORABILIA

Books / Vinyl / Posters
Musical Instruments
Bicycles

IN THE VIRTUAL AGE OF E-BOOKS, MP3 PLAYERS AND DIGITAL CAMERAS, THERE'S STILL A HANKERING FOR THE TOUCH OF PAPER, THE CRACKLE OF VINYL RECORDS OR THE MYSTERY OF ROLLS OF FILM. WITH FRANCE'S STRONG CULTURAL HERITAGE, PARIS HAS PLENTY ON OFFER WHETHER YOU JUST WANT A CHEAP PAPERBACK OR TO DELVE INTO HISTORY THROUGH OLD NEWSPAPERS AND DOCUMENTS.

"Every passion verges on chaos," wrote German philosopher Walter Benjamin in his essay *Unpacking my Library*, "...but what the collecting passion verges on is a chaos of memories." Benjamin's words resonate today in Paris' countless secondhand bookstores: in some everything is painstakingly organised; in others it feels like you are literally burrowing into the past. This is the country that invented photography and cinema, and as well as antique camera shops and flea market stalls, there are excellent sources of documentary and news photos, DVDs and film posters, while anonymous 19th century daguerreotype portraits can still sometimes be picked up for very little money.

Paris' secondhand book and music stores reflect their *quartiers*. There's still a definably Left Bank spirit in the Latin Quarter, Paris' historic university district, and adjacent St-Germain-des-Prés, the traditional publishing quarter, with antiquarian booksellers gathered around the Jardin du Luxembourg, *bande dessinée* (BD) (comic book) sellers on rue Dante, beatnik record stores and specialists in everything from agitprop to crime novels.

Then there are niche districts: a street that is almost entirely devoted to electric guitars on rue de Douai in Pigalle; cameras along boulevard Beaumarchais; the underground record stores near the Bastille; or the 19th century shopping arcades of the *grands boulevards*, originally places to discover novelties, now a repository for stamps and coins, autographs and books, prints and photos.

€

LA GALCANTE

52 rue de l'Arbre Sec, 75001
01 44 77 87 44
www.lagalcante.com
Mon-Sat 12:00-19:00
M° Louvre-Rivoli

There's something almost moving about reading the yellowed pages of a century-old *Le Journal* or *Le Matin* among the piles at La Galcante, a fascinating receptacle for old newspapers and magazines, some of them dating right back to the French Revolution. Crammed into two rooms of a beautiful 18th century *hôtel particulier*, La Galcante was founded by an ex-journalist in the 1970s. The shop does much of its trade supplying birthday issues: go in with a date and they'll dig out the right issue of *Le Figaro, L'Equipe* or that week's *Paris Match*. Old copies of *Paris Match* and *Time* or the graphic black and white photo covers of 70s issues of *Detective*, fashion magazines, film reviews or obscure art journals, and other, even more mysterious documents, such as firemen's calendars, old comics and catalogues, are piled high. Shelves are stacked to the ceiling with white boxes arranged by date or by intriguingly varied subject, from aeronautics, war and railways to knitting and tennis, the Dreyfus case or Catherine Deneuve.

€€

HIFI VINTAGE

9 rue des Déchargeurs, 75001
01 78 01 08 36
www.hifivintage.eu
Mon-Sat 13:00-19:30
M° Châtelet

Old amps and mics, a neon sign proclaiming 'rock 'n' roll' and a curious relief portrait of Claude François complete with nylon hair set the scene in the window for this double boutique shared with Monster Melodies (see p50). Downstairs, in HiFi Vintage, Christian Grados specialises in repairing and selling old turntables, amps, cassette recorders and accessories, mostly from the 70s and 80s.

€

LIBRAIRIE GILDA

36 rue des Bourdonnais, 75001
01 42 83 60 00
www.librairie-paralleles.com
Mon-Sat 10:00-19:00
M° Châtelet or Pont-Neuf

Hidden on a small street just south of Les Halles, Gilda has become a classic among Parisian bargain hunters. You soon see why, with its huge choice of secondhand books, CDs and DVDs, usually in pretty good condition, and a relaxed atmosphere, where the staff will happily leave you to rummage for hours. At first sight the shop looks chaotic, but it turns out to be surprisingly well organised. The book selection is particularly strong on history and politics as well as novels. Nearby are film DVDs and old singles. And if you think that's all there is then head down to the basement for BDs, TV series on DVD, science fiction, jazz and classical CDs, and even videos for those who still have the requisite players. It's the sort of place where you come looking for a film and leave with a book (or the other way round).

€€

LIBRAIRIE DELAMAIN

155 rue St-Honoré, 75001
01 42 61 48 78
www.librairie-delamain.com
Mon-Sat 10:00-20:00
M° Palais-Royal

This venerable bookshop began under the arcades of the Palais Royal but has been in its present location opposite the Comédie Française theatre for over a century. It's part traditional general bookstore, particularly strong on literature and history; and part antiquarian, where wares might range from a complete set of Voltaire or literary first editions to illustrated children's books.

LIBRAIRIE PARALLÈLES

47 rue St-Honoré, 75001
01 42 33 62 70
www.librairie-paralleles.com
Mon-Sat 10:00-19:00
M° Châtelet

The Librairie Gilda's sibling is right-on and activist: there are new books, used records and a political slant, so that Guy Debord and the Situationists, Kerouac and the Beat Poets take pride of place rather than fiction, along with rock biographies and obscure music magazines. Secondhand records occupy the middle of the shop and secondhand CDs are at the rear, with a wide choice of rock, French pop and blues.

MONSTER MELODIES

9 rue des Déchargeurs, 75001
01 40 28 09 39
www.monstermelodies.fr
Mon-Sat 12:00-19:00
M° Châtelet

The upstairs counterpart to HiFi Vintage (see p48) has a monster selection of the sort of music you or your parents used to listen to in the days of vinyl. Initiates delve through secondhand rock, punk, classical, electro and jazz records, more stock sits unpacked in boxes on the floor, and the ceiling is collaged in a crazy, record-sleeve mosaic of T Rex, Iggy Pop, Pink Floyd *et al.*

O'CD

24 rue Pierre Lescot, 75001
01 42 33 50 72
www.ocd.fr
Mon-Sat 11:00-20:00; Sun 14:00-19:00
M° Les Halles or Etienne-Marcel

A cavernous den of used CDs and DVDs, Blu-ray, video games and some vinyl. It's O for 'occasion' and, as the name suggests, the shop originally focused on music CDs but is now more oriented towards film.

Other locations
12 rue St-Antoine, 75004
26 rue des Ecoles, 75005
46 rue du Commerce, 75015

R.F. CHARLE

17 Galerie Véro Dodat, 75001
01 42 33 38 93
www.rfcharle.com
Tue-Sat 14:00-18:30
M° Louvre

A beautiful shop in the calm entrails of an early 19th century covered shopping arcade, where F. Charle has assembled a priceless array of guitars, along with ukeleles, banjos and violins. His great love is the Selmer gypsy jazz guitar, as played by Django Rheinhardt and manufactured in the 1930s and 40s by Selmer. Pricey, but frequented by many of France's (and elsewhere's) singer-songwriters.

PARIS ACCORDÉON

36 rue de la Lune, 75002
01 43 22 13 48
www.parisaccordeon.com
Tue-Sat 10:30-19:00 (closed 13:00-14:30)
M° Strasbourg St-Denis

Devoted to the instrument beloved of *bal musette* and metro buskers, Paris Accordéon was opened in 1944 by an accordion-playing former miner. It left its original rue Daguerre premises in 2012, and although some of the old villagey charm has been lost, the shop has gained in space. It mainly sells new accordions but also has some secondhand instruments that can run into thousands of euros for fine examples, as well as offering a repair service, recordings, sheet music and lessons if you want to learn how to play.

€

ARCHIVES DE LA PRESSE

51 rue des Archives, 75003
01 42 72 63 93
www.lesarchivesdelapresse.com
Mon/Sat 14:00-19:00; Tue-Fri 10:30-19:00
M° Hôtel de Ville

Appropriately located in the street named after the national archives (housed in beautiful Hôtel de Soubise up the street), this shop devoted to back issues of newspapers and magazines was just meant to be. Here are sought after issues of *Paris Match*, intellectual reviews like *Cahiers du Cinéma* and, given the area's fashion bias, lots of vintage fashion mags, such as *Elle* and *Vogue*, as well as books, posters and a miscellany of department store catalogues.

€€

INTEMPOREL

22 rue St-Martin, 75004
01 42 72 55 41
www.intemporel.com
Tue-Sat 12:00-19:00
M° Hôtel de Ville

It looks like any ordinary poster shop from outside, and the portfolios in the street contain small-scale re-editions (not bad as souvenirs) but, inside, Intemporel is the real thing, with an incredible selection of film posters from early classics to recent releases. Many are available in several versions: perhaps Belmondo in *Le Doulos* or *Une Femme est une Femme* in its French, US or Japanese release; Truffaut and Godard; Gabin as Maigret; Audrey Hepburn having breakfast at Tiffany's; James Bond in Italian; Clint Eastwood in Japanese; or the original *Star Wars*. It's fun to rifle through the posters, but ask if you're looking for something specific, as not everything, especially the large format posters, is on display. There's also a small selection of concert and exhibition posters, and vintage travel adverts from Air France or the rail companies. Reproductions cost around €20, originals mostly between €40 and €400, or more for particular rarities.

Camera Boulevard

Despite (or perhaps because of?) the rise and rise of digital cameras, there's still plenty of interest in analogue photography, as seen in the cluster of camera outfits selling both new and old along boulevard Beaumarchais, Paris' camera row (note that in French *caméra* refers to a movie or video camera and *appareil photo* to a stills camera). The side-by-side trio of **Leica Store**, **Le Moyen Format** and **Le Grand Format** (50, 52, 54 boulevard Beaumarchais, 75011; 01 43 55 24 36; www.legrandformat.com), specialising in, respectively, new and old Leicas, medium-format cameras and large-format cameras, have probably the best on the boulevard, with both new and old stock and accessories, and digital and analogue, including rare imported brands of large-format not found elsewhere.

Across the street, **Odéon Occasions** (73 boulevard Beaumarchais, 75003; 01 48 87 74 54; www.odeon-occasions.com) has a fairly priced range that goes from hefty century-old apparatus to recent digital, via historic 1930s Kodak box Brownies, Leica and Zeiss-Ikon, or France's postwar Foca brand, 70s Canon and Minolta and brands from the Eastern Bloc era. The shop also has equipment like slide projectors and enlargers. Most of the shops on boulevard Beaumarchais open Tuesday to Saturday.

€€

LIBRAIRIE ULYSSE

26 rue St-Louis-en-l'Ile, 75004
01 43 25 17 35
www.ulysse.fr
Tue-Fri 14:00-20:00 (and occasional Sat)
M° Pont-Marie

Catherine Domain founded her travel bookshop after exploring the globe. She stocks a vast array of new and old travel books, ranging from recent publications to antique guides and well-worn travellers' journals, and maps for pretty much anywhere you can think of. It is as much a rendezvous for travellers, would-be explorers and eternal wanderers as it is a bookshop, with meetings, discussions and an apéritif on the first Wednesday of the month (except January), and its own literary prize awarded in Catherine's summer boutique at Hendaye in the Pays Basque.

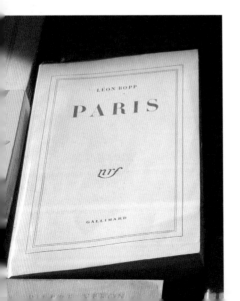

€

MONA LISAIT

17bis rue Pavée, 75004
01 48 87 78 17
www.monalisait.fr
Daily 10:00-20:00
M° St-Paul

With nine branches around Paris, 'Mona was Reading' is mainly known for remainders and reduced-price new books, although it also includes some secondhand books. Once inside, this branch is much larger than you'd expect: a big warehouse space on three levels, including a gallery at the top. All subjects are covered, including cookery, fiction, travel, history and children's books, though it's particularly good for art, including coffee table books, exhibition catalogues and back copies of art magazine *L'Oeil*.

Other locations
9 rue St-Martin, 75004
39 rue Jussieu, 75005

€€

VIRTUOSES DE LA RÉCLAME

5 rue St-Paul, 75004
01 42 72 07 86
www.levillagesaintpaul.com
Tue-Sat 11:00-19:00
M° Pont-Marie

A goldmine of old advertising posters and promotional material, the striking graphic design and nostalgia of old-fashioned brands like La vache qui rit or Dop shampoo. It's mainly posters but also enamel plaques, cardboard cut-outs and other memorabilia.

€€
ANTIQUE CAMÉRAS

6 rue Miromesnil, 75008
01 42 65 27 85
www.antique-cameras.com
Mon-Fri 11:00-18:00
Mº Miromesnil or Champs-Elysées-Clemenceau

Amid the art galleries near the Elysées Palace, Antique Caméras recalls the glory days of rolls of film and legendary names like Rolleiflex and Hasselblad, in an ambience of varnished wood and Agfa film ads, all watched over by Laurel and Hardy cut-outs. Professional photographers and enthusiasts come in for Rolleiflex medium-format TLRs (twin-lens reflex cameras) and their Rolleicord siblings, Zeiss or Leicas, and good condition Nikons. Lenses for Olympus, Pentax, and so on, some with warranties, as well as some recent digital examples, are also sold. Other items are more for collectors, such as vintage large-format cameras, a clutter of early folding Kodaks, and curios like a minuscule metal camera of the sort you might recall from spy movies (sadly, you can't get the film for these any more) or a pen-shaped Stylophot. There are also movie cameras and projectors, antique stereoscopic viewers and cinematic precursors like the zootrope.

€€
LIBRAIRIE D'ART ARTCURIAL

7 Rond-Point des Champs-Elysées, 75008
01 42 99 16 20
www.artcurial.com
Mon-Sat 10:30-19:00
Mº Franklin D Roosevelt

Located in the same splendid premises as auction house Briest-Poulain-F. Tajan (see p130), the Artcurial bookshop is a hub for modern and contemporary art, with an impressive international array of new and out-of-print monographs, and sought-after catalogues raisonnées and exhibition catalogues.

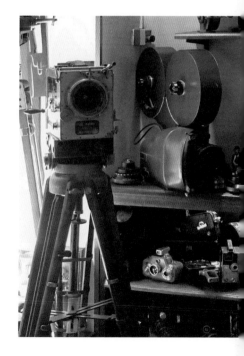

€

AU TROISIÈME OEIL

37 rue de Montholon, 75009
01 48 74 73 17
www.au-troisieme-oeil.com
Mon-Fri 13:00-18:00; Sat 12:00-16:00
M° Cadet

Crime novels and criminology, with a mixture of new and old books, from pulp fiction and fanzines to academic crime studies.

€€

LES CHEMINOTS + ASPHALTE

51 rue de Douai, 75009
01 48 74 33 22
www.lescheminots.fr
Mon 14:00-19:00; Tue-Fri 11:00-19:00;
Sat 10:00-19:00; Sun 11:00-18:00
(closed 12:30-15:00 Sun only)
M° Blanche

One address, two boutiques: Les Cheminots is a *dépôt vente* and repair shop for toy trains, both new and secondhand, with lots of French models but also European brands and railway companies, at numerous scales and gauges, plus rails and scenery; Asphalte specialises in toy cars and motorbikes.

€€

VINTAGE GALLERY

17 boulevard Pereire, 75017
06 09 17 52 50
www.vintagegallery.fr
Tue-Sat 15:00-19:00
M° Malesherbes

Somehow the whole concept of vintage in Paris is inextricably linked with the French fascination for Americana, and such icons as James Dean, the Fonz and Marilyn Monroe. At Vintage Gallery you are in the Technicolor world of 50s Wurlitzer jukeboxes, one-armed bandits and 70s pinball machines, Coca Cola memorabilia, diner furniture and chrome bar stools. There's even a vintage petrol pump to complete the look.

Riff Row

On a Pigalle backstreet, roughly halfway between the rock music venues of boulevard Rochechouart and the *luthiers* (violin makers) of rue de Rome, rue de Douai, and its continuation rue Victor-Massé, is where rock musicians, aspiring rock musicians and groupies come for a string of specialist guitar shops, instruments galore and all the amps, pedals and accessories to go with them. **Central Guitars** (12 rue de Douai; 01 42 81 13 15; www.centraleguitars.com), the first to set up on the stretch, now has four shops devoted to acoustic and electric guitars, bass guitars and rare guitars. There are plenty of famous names like Gibson, Fender and Taylor and the chance to discover lesser-known brands such as French-made LAG.

Le Guitar Store (No.11; 01 48 74 08 80; www.guitarstore.fr) has new and used, with stratospheric prices for some prized vintage. Similarly, **Le Guitarium** (No.9; 01 55 32 26 59; www.leguitarium.fr) has new and used vintage Gibson and Fender guitars, alongside secondhand amps, while **Oldies Guitars** (31 rue Victor-Massé; 01 42 80 93 66; www.oldies-guitars.com) sells acoustic and electric, including secondhand and re-edited vintage models.

Covered Passages

A forerunner of the great department stores, Paris' picturesque 19th century covered shopping arcades allowed Parisians to discover novelties free from rain, the clatter of horse carriages and the dirt of the streets that didn't yet have pavements. Today it's less novelties and more receptacles of curios and eccentric wine bars, but they still form a world all of their own, with their glass roofs, mosaic floors, period shopfronts and tiny staircases leading up to mysterious reserves or apartments.

The **Passage des Panoramas** (11 boulevard Montmartre/10 rue St-Marc), opened in 1800 with two cylindrical towers where panoramic views of foreign capitals were projected (foreshadowing the arrival of cinema), has been colonised today by stamp and coin dealers, and tiny bistros and wine bars, like fashionable Racines and Coinstot Bistro. **Autographes Arnaud Magistry** (No.60; 01 40 41 12 18; www.magistry-autographes.com) specialises in old autographs and documents; perhaps a letter from Delacroix or Picasso, a scientist or politician, or signed photos of actors, recent pop stars and even footballers. It's stamps at **La Postale** (No.55; 01 40 26 63 03; www.la-postale-philatelie.fr) and **Marigny Philatelie** (No.9; 01 40 39 06 74; www.marigny-philatelie.com), and the lost world of old postcards at **Maréchal** (No.14; 01 42 36 09 46; www.cartespostalesdecollection.com).

Across the boulevard, **Passage Jouffroy** (10 boulevard Montmartre/9 rue de la Grange-Batalière) is home to Grévin (the Paris waxworks), the eccentric, inexpensive Hôtel Chopin, and Café Zephyr, complete with billiards table. **M.G.W. Segas** (No.34; 01 47 70 89 65; www.canesegas.com) epitomises the appeal of the arcades, the allure of a cabinet of curiosities, where behind stylish window displays there is a shrine to the walking stick, many of them beautifully carved objects with bone or silver heads. Just opposite, the child is king at **Librairie Le Petit Roi** (No.39; 01 40 22 94 60), devoted to BDs and children's books. If many, like vintage *Mickey*, first editions of *Tintin*, or the Breton maid *Bécassine*, who first appeared in the 1920s, appeal most to adult collectors, there's also an inexpensive pile of series like *Geronimo Stilton* and *Tom Tom et Nana* that kids are actually reading today. Around the corner, **Librairie du Passage** (Nos.48-62; 01 56 03 94 10) stretches along the passage with a fabulous variety of new and used books on art, particularly the decorative arts. **Photo Verdeau** (No.47; 01 47 70 51 91; www.verdeau.com) has changing photo shows and a colossal reserve of photographs neatly arranged in boxes to file through, from 19th century albumen prints and 20th century documentary photographers to recent images and a box of odds and ends sold for one euro a piece. Along with a few well-known photographers like Doisneau, Jeanloup Sieff, Josef Siduc, Willy Ronis and Robert Capa, or portraits of film stars, are many more anonymous portraits, mountain landscapes, family groups and documentary images that recall the construction of the Paris metro in the early 1900s, or colonial-era photos of India and Morocco.

Jouffroy's continuation, **Passage Verdeau** (56 rue de la Grange-Batelière/31 bis rue Montmartre), is like an overflow of Quartier Drouot antiques district, with its small galleries and booksellers. **Librairie Roland Buret** (No.6; 01 47 70 62 99) specialises in children's books, BDs and *Astérix* figurines. **Librairie La Farfouille** (No.27; 01 47 70 21 15; www.farfouille. fr) is packed with eclectic history and memoirs, obscure almanacs and political speeches, biographies, literature and fine art books, with prices from a few euros to several hundred for rare first editions. At **Galerie Valence** (No.22; 01 42 47 06 79; www.galerie-valence.com), Pierre de Valence has a collector's magpie eye as he welcomes you in to show you wares ranging from 18th century furniture, directoire chairs, a terracotta bust, antique clocks and candle snuffers to a pair of intriguing 1930s armchairs – or as he describes it all, "A boutique dreamed like a family home."

€

BANCO CASH

37 boulevard Voltaire, 75011
01 48 05 25 42
www.banco-cash.com
Tue-Sat 10:00-19:00 (closed 13:00-14:00)
Mº Oberkampf

The look is hardly auspicious and the slogan simply 'we buy cash,' but Banco Cash is a useful source of cast-off wind instruments, guitars, hi-fi and computer games, old skateboards and roller skates. Not the lowest for prices, but all objects are tested and come with a guarantee. The branch in the 12th arrondissement focuses on computers.

Other location
203 rue de Charenton, 75012

€

BORN BAD

17 rue Keller, 75011
01 43 38 41 78
www.bornbad.fr
Mon-Sat 12:00-20:00
Mº Ledru-Rollin or Bastille

Bad music for bad people with a vibe that goes back to the heady days of punk. The records and CDs here include lots of punk, indie and garage, but also take in recent bands and 50s rock 'n' roll, as well as re-releases and compilations on the shop's own label. A good place to find flyers too.

€€

BIMBO TOWER

5 passage St-Antoine, 75011
01 49 29 76 70
http://bimbo.tower.free.fr
Mon-Fri 13:00-19:00; Sat 11:00-19:00
Mº Ledru-Rollin

This place probably qualifies as Paris' weirdest record store, dedicated to underground sound, electronica, lo-fi, post-punk, Japanese underground and much more. CDs, secondhand records and re-editions are complemented by obscure magazines, fanzines, criticism, T-shirts and miscellaneous cardboard objects.

€ - €€

LULU BERLU

2 rue du Grand-Prieuré, 75011
01 43 55 12 52
www.lulu-berlu.com
Mon-Sat 11:00-19:30 (July-Aug 12:00-19:00)
Mº Oberkampf

Whereas many secondhand toyshops are deeply serious collectors' affairs, at Lulu Berlu, which claims to be France's largest shop of collectors' toys, the items look as if they could actually be played with. The emphasis, apart from a few soft toys, is firmly in a mass-market world (and several fellow planets) of cheerfully colourful plastic. There are My Little Ponies; Action Men; collectors' Barbies; a village-full of Smurfs (known in France as Schtroumpfs); Britains' cowboys, horses, farm animals and guardsmen; and French counterpart Starlux, for Roman gladiators, more cowboys and Indians, dinosaurs and even French Revolutionary figures. Then there are masses of *Star Wars* figurines and space capsules, often still in their original packaging; Captain Scarlet and his cohorts; and more intergalactic heroes than one could ever remember, as well as some episodes of popular culture surely better forgotten – Pamela Anderson dolls anyone?

€

MINIBUS

4 rue Monte Cristo, 75020
www.minibuspetitbazarvintage.blogspot.com
Wed-Sat 11:00-19:00 (closed Aug)
Mº Alexandre Dumas

Minibus is a mini-boutique. Lore Bargès, singer in musical duo Dragibus, which performs experimental electro songs for children, has amassed a tempting retro array of children's toys, educational games and storybooks. Many come from vintage job lots and old manufacturers' stocks so there's an amusing mix of old school exercise books and satchels, plastic ducks, rattles, lotto games, buckets and spades, dolls or robots.

€€

LES POUPÉES D'AUTREFOIS

116 avenue Parmentier, 75011
01 43 55 35 71
www.lespoupeesdautrefois.com
Mon-Fri 14:00-18:30 (or by appointment)
Mº Parmentier

'Dolls from Yesteryear' has a huge assortment of dolls, from antique china dolls, baby dolls and the line of dolls marketed by *Modes et Travaux* magazine since the 50s to Barbie and Midge. Also has its own repair workshop.

LATIN QUARTER

€€

AAAPOUM BAPOUM

8 rue Dante, 75005
01 43 25 09 37
www.aaablog.typepad.com
Mon-Sat 11:00-20:00
M° Cluny-La Sorbonne or St-Michel

'Thwack,' 'zzzz,' 'biff'... a den for lovers of BDs and manga, with a range that goes from discount boxes out front to rare tomes, and many regulars who pop in for that missing volume. The shop's blog mixes humour, erudition and self-deprecation and there's the same mood here in the shop itself, in what they themselves describe as "apparent disorder." *Tintin* and *Hoppy the Kangaroo*, *Tarzan* comics, French and Belgian classics, American heroes, old copies of *Marvel Comics*, and great illustrators like Moebius and Robert Crumb are arranged in wooden Bordeaux wine cases; there's even a section devoted to Clint Eastwood, who, it turns out, was a 60s comic book hero.

Other location
14 rue Serpente, 75006

€

ABBEY BOOKSHOP

29 rue de la Parcheminerie, 75005
01 46 33 16 24,
Mon-Sat 10:00-19:00
M° Cluny-La Sorbonne

Behind a beautiful rococo housefront on a narrow medieval Latin Quarter street, the Abbey Bookshop was opened over 20 years ago by Canadian Brian Spence, who keeps the Maple Leaf flying above the door, and includes some Québecois titles in French amid the largely English-language books. Regular book launches and readings help keep things animated. There's some new and lots of secondhand, stacked in perilous piles and crammed into boxes, though once you manage to squeeze inside, the shop is surprisingly deep. Particularly good on French and modern history, literature and classics.

€

L'AMOUR DU NOIR

11 rue du Cardinal-Lemoine, 75005
01 43 29 25 66
http://amourdunoir.pagesperso-orange.fr
Daily 12:00-19:00
M° Cardinal-Lemoine

You have to sleuth this place out with its easy-to-miss black (of course) facade, but inside is a meticulously arranged secondhand bookshop devoted to the dark world of *polars* (crime novels). Most are inexpensive paperbacks, including the famous Série Noire detective and mystery series, 1950s and 60s La Fleuve Noire titles tempting for their striking graphic covers, or famous names like Agatha Christie and Léo Malet. Then there is the chance for discoveries like Henri Catalan's detective nun Soeur Angèle. There's also sci-fi and fantasy, a shelf of vampire titles, a case of first editions and back issues of erudite film review *Cahiers du Cinéma*. The shop attracts a mix of idle browsers and those in search of a missing title, and is conveniently close to both the BiLiPo, library of crime literature (at No.48), and the mysterious Paris Police Museum hidden inside an ugly police station (4 rue de la Montagne Ste-Geneviève).

€

BOULINIER

20 boulevard St-Michel, 75006
01 43 26 90 57
www.boulinier.com
Mon/Fri/Sat 10:00-00:00; Tue-Thu 10:00-23:00; Sun 14:00-00:00
M° Cluny-La Sorbonne, Odéon or St-Michel

Boulinier has been selling books on the boulevard since 1845, and its four-level maze still always seems to be full of bargain hunters, fervently shuffling through the racks in hope of a happy find. On the first floor it's vinyl LPs and singles, CDs, music and film DVDs; the second floor is BDs, the only section that is largely new; the basement has books; and there are bargain boxes of paperbacks for as little as 20 centimes on the pavement outside. Leave plenty of time, as things are only loosely – and not always reliably – categorised, but there's something addictive about this place, and with prices so low it's almost impossible not to leave with something.

€€
CINÉ CORNER

1 rue de l'Ecole de Médicine, 75006
01 43 26 17 13
www.cine-corner-paris.fr
Mon-Fri 11:00-19:30; Sat 10:00-19:30
M° Cluny-La Sorbonne

This tiny scarlet boutique is a haunt of
film buffs in search of secondhand DVDs
and Blu-ray. Unlike nearby Boulinier (see
p63), here everything is meticulously
arranged and classified by director or
genre, and although it's small, the shop
has an admirably wide-ranging selection,
strong on art-house movies, legendary
actors, obscure horror and Japanese
directors.

€
CROCODISC

40 and 42 rue des Ecoles, 75005
01 43 54 33 22
www.crocodisc.com
Tue-Sat 11:00-19:00 (closed Aug)
M° Cluny-La Sorbonne

Side-by-side boutiques for lovers of vinyl: at
No.40 it's soul, R & B, funk, reggae, salsa and
world music; at No.42 British and American
rock, French pop, prog rock, folk, a little
electro and rarities such as whole boxes
of film soundtracks – in fact, as they put it,
"everything but classical" (though the odd
classical record slips in too). There are also
CDs and music DVDs, but it is the records
that are the real point, with everything well
organised and sleeves in plastic covers.
Crocodisc has been here since 1978 and still
has something of the ambience of the days
of punk and indie, with staff who are happy
to help or let you browse in a memory trip
to the days of Marc Almond, Depeche Mode
and Ziggy Stardust.

€
CROCOJAZZ

64 rue de la Montagne-Sainte-Geneviève,
75005
01 46 34 78 38
www.crocodisc.com
Tue-Sat 11:00-19:00
(closed late July/early Aug)
M° Maubert-Mutualité or Cardinal Lemoine

The sibling of Crocodisc, up the hill
opposite La Dame Blanche, is devoted to
jazz, blues, gospel and crooners.

ETAT D'ORIGINE

5 rue St-Victor, 75005
01 43 25 67 66
Tue-Sat 14:00-19:00 (closed Aug)
M° Maubert-Mutualité

This tiny shop is mainly devoted to old train sets and toy cars, but alongside prized Dinky *et al.* you'll also find less precious plastic roundabouts, model cowboys and some amusing throwbacks to childhood, like deliciously kitsch *Dukes of Hazard* or Goofy lunchboxes.

€

GEPETTO & VÉLOS

59 rue du Cardinal-Lemoine, 75005
01 43 54 19 95
www.gepetto-velos.com
Tue-Sat 09:00-19:30; Sun 10:00-19:00
(closed daily 13:00-15:00; closed Sun in Jan and Feb)
M° Cardinal-Lemoine

There's always a row of secondhand bikes lined up on the pavement outside Gepetto & Vélos, a used bike seller, and although they do sell new Dutch, French and American town bikes, mountain bikes, electrically assisted bikes and folding bikes, the real interest lies in the pre-loved selection, with excellent prices if you're looking for a sturdy black number for pedalling around town. Fouad and Annemarie, the couple who run the shop, also rent the bikes out, run bike tours and carry out repairs; used by everyone in the area when they've got a flat tyre or want their chain replaced.

€ €

LA DAME BLANCHE

47 rue de la Montagne-Sainte-Geneviève, 75005
01 43 54 54 45
Mon-Sat 10:30-19:30; Sun 11:30-20:00
M° Maubert-Mutualité or Cardinal-Lemoine

This small shop climbing up the hill towards the Panthéon has an impressive choice of new and old classical CDs, plus records in boxes at the front. Be prepared to sift your way through the boxes, although the friendly owner will produce a stool as you finger through those on the ground, and check the promotions boxes for good deals. There are sections devoted to Baroque and opera and a good selection of avant-garde composers – if you're after a recording by Xenakis or cult 'concrète music' composer Pierre Henry, then the chances are you'll find it here.

€

GIBERT JOSEPH

26-34 boulevard St-Michel, 75006
01 44 41 88 88
www.gibertjoseph.com
Mon-Sat 10:00-20:00
M° Cluny-La Sorbonne

This big Latin Quarter university and
general bookshop, selling everything
from comic books to school textbooks,
guidebooks and scholarly tomes, is
unusual in that secondhand books are
displayed alongside new ones, which is
useful when you want to compare prices
or pick up a barely touched bestseller, a
classic text or the latest teen read, and
with its buy and sell policy, many of the
secondhand books are virtually new.
Occupying a long stretch of boulevard
St-Michel, there are seven floors of books
at No.26 and three floors of new and
secondhand CDs and DVDs at No.34.

€ €

RACKHAM

2 rue Dante, 75005
01 56 24 49 00
Tue-Sat 10:00-20:00
M° Cluny-La Sorbonne or St-Michel

This specialist in secondhand *bandes
dessinées* is named after Red Rackham,
the pirate in the *Tintin* stories, so there
are all the *Tintins* you'd expect, along
with plenty of other fodder for serious
collectors and rarities locked away in
glass cases. It has a reputation as snooty
and expensive but the choice is huge and
the condition of the BDs is good.

LIBRAIRIE MICHAEL SEKSIK

€ €

8 rue Lacépède, 75005
01 43 43 53 53
www.librairiemichaelseksik.com
Mon-Sat 10:00-19:00
M° Place Monge

With books, posters and prints, Seksik has all you need of a good secondhand bookshop, but the real discovery here is the posters, concert flyers and documents from the era of 60s and 70s psychedelia and May 68 agitprop, assembled by Michael Seksik, who scours the world for posters, and associate Stéphane Schoufliker, who generally mans the shop.

The owners confirm that the underlying theme of the shop is "illustration". "Compared to the craze for vintage furniture, the graphic art of the period has been curiously forgotten," says Stéphane, pointing out how the striking curvilinear, psychedelic forms of 70s American poster artists were inspired by the curves of Art Nouveau. "These posters were often printed in great quantity – they were plastered all over the place – but it's difficult to find them in good condition." Most come from Britain, France or the US, with concert posters for the Beatles, Herman's Hermits and the Grateful Dead, and political posters like an anti-Vietnam notice for a meeting in the Latin Quarter. They also sell some of the original artwork for the posters. Don't ignore the books either – art and photography, children's literature, including illustrated French and English classics, criminology and recent novels – and rifle through the folder of prints that might include 1880s photographs, caricatures and period board games.

LATIN QUARTER BITES

gourmet cooking with lots of tiny tasting dishes and mysterious herbs

LE PRÉ VERRE

8 rue Thénard, 75005
01 43 54 59 47
www.lepreverre.com

This Latin Quarter bistro is always busy for its bargain daily lunch menu. Fresh market cooking is combined with chef Philippe Delacourcelle's imaginative use of spices. Ideal before browsing the *quartier's* comic book shops and record stores.

€€
SHAKESPEARE AND CO

37 rue de la Bûcherie, 75005
01 43 25 40 93
www.shakespeareandcompany.com
Mon-Fri 10:00-23:00; Sat/Sun 11:00-23:00
M° St-Michel

Shakespeare and Co has become part of the Left Bank literary myth; sightseers work their way through the maze of small rooms and gawp as much at the readers sprawled on sofas as the books piled up to the rafters. Founded by American-in-Paris George Whitman in the 1950s and named after the mythic Parisian bookshop in rue de l'Odéon, where Sylvia Beach first published James Joyce's *Ulysses* in 1922, there's a huge choice of new and used literature, an antiquarian section next door and the upstairs 'library', where you can read the much-thumbed books from Whitman's own personal collection. Since being taken over by George's daughter, Sylvia Whitman, the shop has modernised a little with a telephone and a website, a busy programme of events, readings and literary workshops, but it still serves as a boarding house for aspiring writers who stay for a few days or several months in search of the literary muse.

€€
LA TORTUE ELECTRIQUE

7 rue Frédéric-Sauton, 75005
01 43 29 37 08
www.tortueelectrique.org
Tue-Sat 14:00-18:00
M° Maubert-Mutualité

Perhaps it should be called the 'eclectic tortoise', with its collection of old toys that range from 19th century *jeu de l'oie* board games (the goose game, a little like snakes and ladders) and antique playing cards that are practically historic documents to more whimsical glove puppets and a flock of painted clockwork birds made from tin. Well worth a look, although the owner, Georges Monnier, is more welcoming to serious collectors than casual passers-by.

ST-GERMAIN-DES-PRÉS/MONTPARNASSE

€€
ANTIQ PHOTO

16 rue de Vaugirard, 75006
01 46 33 83 27
www.antiq-photo.com
Tue-Sat 14:00-19:00
M° Odéon or RER Luxembourg

Walking in here is a bit like entering a
timewarp laboratory. As well as antique
cameras and early movie cameras,
and pre-cinema magic lanterns, stereo
viewers and other optical devices, there
are all sorts of antiquated scientific and
astronomical instruments, microscopes
and measuring apparatus, and even
curious medical equipment. The shop also
sells early photographs, daguerrotype
portraits, photographic plates and
stereoscopic images and projectors.

€€
LA CHAMBRE CLAIRE/
LIBRAIRIE CONTACTS

14 rue St-Sulpice, 75006
01 46 34 04 31 (photography)
01 43 59 17 71 (cinema)
www.la-chambre-claire.fr
Tue-Sat 11:00-19:00
M° Odéon

Two specialist bookshops with an
international range of new and out-
of-print titles: La Chambre Claire
specialises in photography books, along
with changing photo exhibitions, while
Contacts is devoted to cinema and the
moving image.

€€

LA CHAUMIÈRE À MUSIQUE

5 rue de Vaugirard, 75006
01 43 54 07 25
www.la-chaumiere-a-musique.fr
Mon-Fri 10:00-19:30; Sat 10:00-20:00
Sun 14:00-20:00
M° Odéon or RER Luxembourg

A small shop with a huge choice of secondhand-only classical CDs and DVDs, knowledgeable staff and a serious atmosphere.

€€€

CINE IMAGES

68 rue de Babylone, 75007
01 47 05 60 25
www.cine-images.com
Tue-Fri 10:00-19:00 (closed 13:00-14:00);
Sat 14:00-19:00 (closed Aug)
M° Vaneau

Situated opposite the Japanese-style La Pagode cinema, Cine Images displays film posters in the manner of a gallery, with pride of place given to a Hollywoodian golden age of the 40s to 60s, and to the days of striking graphic art, but also to French *nouvelle vague* directors, stars like Jean Gabin and Fernandel, Bond and Cinecitta. The shop also has a collection of film stills, portraits and press photos.

€€

LIBRAIRIE CINÉ REFLET

14 rue Monsieur-le-Prince, 75006
01 40 46 02 72,
www.cinereflet.fr
Mon-Sat 13:00-20:00
M° Odéon

This cinema bookshop is a must for cinephiles, with an incredible choice of new and old biographies, film criticism, theory, back issues of *Cahiers du Cinéma*, *Première* and *Sight and Sound*, posters, press dossiers and screenplays.

€€ LIBRAIRIE LE PONT TRAVERSE

62 rue de Vaugirard, 75006
01 45 48 06 48
Tue-Fri 12:00-19:00; Sat 15:00-19:00
M° St-Sulpice

Behind the wrought-iron and painted glass facade of a pretty belle époque butcher's shop, the secondhand bookstore founded by poet and painter Marcel Béalu, a friend of the Surrealists, has preserved its Surrealist touch in a magpie array of rare editions, illustrated books, art, poetry, literature and prints.

€ OXFAM LA BOUQUINERIE

61 rue Daguerre, 75014
01 42 79 83 10
www.oxfamfrance.org
Tue-Sat 11:00-19:00; Sun 10:30-13:30
M° Denfert-Rochereau

This recent British import – selling secondhand books, CDs and DVDs – is run by volunteers and raises money for Oxfam. Children's storytelling sessions are held on Wednesday afternoons.

Other location
8 rue St-Ambroise, 75011

€€ PALEOPHONIES

16 rue de Vaugirard, 75006
01 46 33 20 17
www.pong-story.com/paleophonies
Tue-Sat 13:00-19:00 (closed Aug)
M° Odéon or RER Luxembourg

Paleophonies offers a fascinating trip back to the days when radios were called wirelesses and took up half the room. Shopkeeper David Winter is fanatical – and knowledgeable – about what he calls *antiquités sonores*, amassing a fantastic array of vintage radios, early TVs, record players and old tape recorders, as well as a stock of the needles, lamps, etc. required to make them work. As well as buying and selling, he also carries out repairs and rents items out.

€

UN REGARD MODERNE

10 rue Gît-le-Coeur, 75006
01 43 29 13 93
Mon-Sat 11:30-20:00
M° St-Michel

This cult beatnik bookshop is an extraordinary vision of organised chaos, with so many precarious piles of books you can barely get inside for fear of cascading volumes and the near impossibility of finding anything amid the wealth of underground literature, art and film books, criticism, and obscure writings. Fortunately, chaos is combined with personal service, and owner Jacques Noël seems to remember exactly where things are. If you ask for a particular subject, perhaps Dada and Duchamp (it certainly feels surreal) or the Beat Poets, who just happened to stay at the hotel down the street, he'll immediately climb up on a ladder and fetch down a dozen relevant books.

€€

SAN FRANCISCO BOOK COMPANY

17 rue Monsieur le Prince, 75006
01 43 29 15 70
www.sanfranciscobooksparis.com
Mon-Sat 11:00-21:00; Sun 14:00-19:30
M° Odéon

This stalwart among Paris' English-language secondhand bookshops is a civilised intellectual haunt, good for those after the classic Parisian literary expats, but also with a wealth of other books from literary first editions, poetry and art books to quantities of used paperbacks. They buy as well as sell, but are carefully selective with what they take.

HOME & INTERIORS

Home Furnishings / Décor
Lighting / Salvage

FRANCE'S FABULOUS HERITAGE OF AVANT-GARDE DESIGN AND DECORATIVE ARTS MAKES PARIS A WONDERFUL HUNTING GROUND FOR FURNITURE AND HOUSEHOLD ITEMS, WHETHER IT'S A QUESTION OF SEEKING OUT PRECIOUS ART OBJECTS OR AN AMUSING MEMORY TRIP THROUGH OLD KITCHEN GADGETS.

Here it seems to be particularly true that not only is one man's junk another's treasure, but also that yesterday's junk is today's treasure; once neglected pieces of avant-garde furniture from the 50s and 60s, by designers like Jean Prouvé and Charlotte Perriand, have become the sought-after collector's items of today's international art market. Happily you can still find affordable pieces, as the fashion for vintage has spread to unnamed pieces of French and Scandinavian design and the fun colours and patterns of Formica and 60s kitchen china. On one hand they meet the practicalities of furniture made for today's lifestyle in small houses and apartments, rather than the massive wardrobes and commodes of the 19th century, and on the other they have the appeal of an era that spelled optimism and modernity.

As well as numerous vintage furniture specialists at the Puces de St-Ouen, especially at the Marché Paul-Bert (see p116), it's no surprise that many of the

top-of-the-market specialist galleries have set up amid the art galleries of St-Germain. More offbeat *brocantes* with a nostalgic touch abound in bohemian Batignolles and Montmartre, while a flea market-like cluster of friendly secondhand shops is growing up around rue du Marché Popincourt. Then there are the massive *dépôt ventes* where you'll find entire house clearances and dining ensembles, or recycling and recuperation specialists, where *brocanteurs* restore and adapt, bringing secondhand furniture back to life.

€€

GALERIE ALEXIS LAHELLEC

14-16 rue Jean-Jacques-Rousseau, 75001
01 42 33 36 95
www.alexislahellec.com
Mon-Sat 12:00-19:00
M° Palais-Royal

Alexis Lahellec has gone through a number of reincarnations since the days of his kitsch knick-knack shops, Why!, via costume jewellery designer, and has arrived at this showroom near Palais Royal, devoted to the sort of vintage furniture he has collected for 30 years. There's a wide range of vintage chairs, Scandinavian sideboards and rosewood chests of drawers, leather sofas and armchairs, *très* 70s bamboo chairs by Viggo Boesen, and a few discoveries that make the difference, like a pile of 1965 Albinson stacking chairs by the unjustly forgotten Don Albinson, long-serving chief designer for Eames and Knoll.

€€

L'OEIL DU PÉLICAN

13 rue Jean-Jacques-Rousseau, 75001
01 40 13 70 00
www.loeildupelican.fr
Tue-Fri 11:00-18:30; Sat 15:30-18:30
M° Palais-Royal

One of a dying breed of dusty old *brocantes*, where the owner's pelican eye (it's on the corner of rue du Pélican) extends from some genuine antiques to a bit of 20th century, lots of junk and curios that really are curious. The disorder is almost irresistible; you might come across an 18th century gilt mirror, an unusual wooden lamp, old enamel advertising plaques and engravings, wooden storks, a Barbotine Faience duck jug (she clearly has something about birds), a leather riding boot (no sign of the second) and little wooden display cases containing everything from watches to old pill boxes.

€€

AU BON USAGE

21 rue St-Paul, 75004
01 42 78 80 14
www.aubonusage.com
Wed-Mon 11:00-19:00
M° St-Paul or Sully-Morland

This small shop is cluttered with bentwood furniture by German furniture maker Michael Thonet and his followers, from the basic chairs, which were early pioneers of mass production and have furnished countless bistros, to more fanciful curlicue extravaganzas of coat stands, rocking chairs and chaises longues. Most are newly re-caned, and sold in an atmosphere of dark wood and polish.

€

AU PETIT BONHEUR LA CHANCE

13 rue St-Paul, 75004
01 42 74 36 38
www.levillagesaintpaul.com
Thu-Mon 11:00-19:00 (closed 13:00-14:30)
M° St-Paul or Sully-Morland

In the Village St-Paul, a Marais enclave of antique shops and artists' studios, the 'happy find' is a nostalgic housewife's corner of old educational posters and school exercise books, rubbers and pots of glue. There are advertising tins for old-fashioned drinks like Banania, neat piles of linen tea towels, flour boxes and stacks of bowls for drinking hot chocolate or *café au lait* in the morning, with some good decoration finds, like old enamelled street and room numbers, among what can verge on twee.

€

AUX COMPTOIRS DU CHINEUR

49 rue St-Paul, 75004
01 42 72 47 39
Tue-Sun 14:00-20:30
M° St-Paul

Whereas most of the rue St-Paul enclave is sedate and organised, here it is cheerfully junky: a cacophony of household items and accessories, with stiletto shoes next to orange 60s lamps, old records and telephones, and lots of hats and kitchen clocks. It's as if the owner simply cannot resist piling in everything he likes, taking you on a walk down memory lane with fun finds next to horrors and music playing on the jukebox as you sift your way through the debris.

€€

CASSIOPÉE

Village St-Paul (in courtyard), 23-25 rue St-Paul, 75004
01 42 74 00 45
www.levillagesaintpaul.com
Thu-Mon 11:00-19:00
M° St-Paul

Cassiopée is one of the stalwarts of the Village St-Paul enclave, piled high with classy glass, silver and tableware, or as the French call it *les arts de la table*. There are complete porcelain dinner services, silverware that ranges from bundles of forks to flamboyant champagne buckets and other table accessories, but it's really best for glassware, with shelves of wine glasses and decanters, coloured Bohemian glass and Lorraine manufacturers like Baccarat, St-Louis and Daum.

€€

GALERIE ANDERS HUS

27 rue Charlot, 75003
01 42 72 00 49
www.andershus.fr
Wed-Sat 14:00-19:00
M° St-Sébastien-Froissart

Along with the Galerie Dansk next door (see p80), this stretch of rue Charlot has become a little corner of Scandinavia. Here Anders Lausten has gathered all the 20th century arts: oil paintings, furniture, glass, Poulsen lamps and a superb selection of Scandinavian art pottery and ceramics, with some inexpensive vases in among known names.

€€

GALERIE BALOUGA

25 rue des Filles du Calvaire
01 42 74 01 49
www.balouga.com
Tue-Fri 12:30-19:00; Sat 14:00-19:00
M° Filles du Calvaire

The fashion for mid-century design has extended to kids, and in this gallery it's fascinating to discover that many of the now-cult furniture designs were also produced in mini-models for children: with scaled-down versions of the metal-grid Bertoia chair, colourful red 50s American chairs and others by Eames, Jacobsen and Kartell, as well as 50s desks and re-edited pieces, some young designers and Balouga's own creations.

€€

GALERIE DANSK

31 rue Charlot, 75003
01 42 71 45 95
www.galeriedansk.com
Tue-Sat 14:00-19:00
Mº St-Sébastien-Froissart

A tribute to the days when Scandinavian spelled modern, with its simple lines and good craftsmanship. Classics of Danish design from the 50s to the 70s – Arne Jacobsen chairs, rosewood sideboards, spiky suspension lamps – are displayed against the exposed stone walls of a historic Marais building.

€€

HIER POUR DEMAIN

4 rue des Francs-Bourgeois, 75003
01 42 78 14 29
www.antiquites-hierpourdemain.com
Tue-Sat 13:00-19:00; Sun/Mon 14:00-19:00
Mº St-Paul

Like many places, 'Yesterday for Tomorrow', having previously focused on art deco, has followed the trend for 1950s and 60s furniture, with an appealingly domestic array of colourful sideboards, boomerang coffee tables and wrought-iron magazine racks. Chairs and sofas, cheerfully reupholstered in re-editions of 50s graphic-patterned printed fabrics now have the air of a vintage ideal home advertisement. There's also a good selection of colourful Bakelite bracelets and brooches and those painted glass tumblers made for summer drinks.

€€

MERCI

111 boulevard Beaumarchais, 75003
01 42 77 00 33
www.merci-merci.com
Mon-Sat 10:00-19:00
M° St-Sébastien-Froissart

If Colette was the lifestyle store that
marked the 1990s, then Merci, which
opened in 2009 over three floors of an
artfully converted industrial building
on the edge of the Marais, is proof that
secondhand is chic. A finger-on-the-
pulse mix of highly desirable casual
new fashion, designer furniture and
housewares is intermingled with a wily
selection of vintage pieces. Prices are
high but you can take comfort in the
knowledge that some of the profits go to
a development charity in Madagascar.
The secondhand furniture, in particular,
doesn't just follow fads but is brilliantly
eclectic; perhaps a metal garden bench,
Formica kitchen table or grey Gustavian
dining chairs, where the distressed look
is key. In addition, the tea room doubles
as secondhand bookstore, where you can
browse its shelves of books over cakes
and tea.

€€€

MOBILIER 54

54-56 rue Charlot, 75003
01 44 61 31 13
www.mobilier54.com
Tue-Sat 11:00-19:00
M° St-Sébastien-Froissart

Dedicated to the international design look, well-curated, pricey, 50s-70s furniture from the classic manufacturers – Eames chairs for Herman Miller, Jacobsen for Fritz Hansen, Knoll sideboards and tables – is shown off in a gallery setting. But what could be just a conventional greatest hits selection is enlivened by objects and accessories that complete the look, such as ashtrays, heavy 1950s glass vases or Ray-Ban sunglasses. There are some interesting oddities alongside the famous names, such as a 70s coat rack that looks more like a Courrèges dress, or the leather and metal Banc Beaubourg (row of seats), supported on a heavy steel joist, which was originally designed for the Centre Pompidou in 1977.

€€

(RE)SOURCE

7 rue de Turenne, 75004
01 44 61 09 60
Tue-Sun 11:00-20:00
M° Bastille or St-Paul

This tiny two-storey space opposite Delphine Pariente (see p18) cleverly pairs menswear – vintage leather jackets and new T-shirts and bags – with vintage furniture, hunted out by the owner. The selection changes frequently, going for laidback 50s mood – a 50s wooden secretaire desk, Scandinavian sideboard, assorted 50s vases and ashtrays, and a slick leather-covered portable TV – and reasonable prices rather than known names.

€

BROCANTE DES BATIGNOLLES

16 rue Brochant, 75017
09 53 01 23 61
www.brocantedesbatignolles.com
Tue-Fri 13:00-19:00; Sat 10:30-19:00
M° Brochant

All you need for perfecting nostalgia in your kitchen with a homely selection of old tin advertising plaques and boxes, graphic 1970s teasets, enamelled tin coffee pots and storage jars (farine, thé, café, etc.), old saucepans and piles of old colanders, accompanied by the occasional clockwork toy. It's picturesque though not a bargain.

€€

CHEZ 1962/ GALERIE 1962

3 and 4 rue Tholozé, 75018
01 42 54 28 08
www.boutique1962.com
Tue-Sat 10:30-19:30
M° Abbesses or Blanche

Back to the 60s of orange, lime green and duck egg blue. Colour and pattern prime in the duo of boutiques created by Catherine Lupis Thomas, where an amusing selection of 1950s and 60s furniture is cleverly displayed amid colourful new vintage-inspired – or never-ceased production – fashion, accessories, patterned mugs and graphic furnishing fabrics designed by Orla Kiely, Marimekko, Mellow Yellow, Missprint and other cult European brands. The attitude to the past is affectionate but not too serious. One shop is focused more on clothes, the other more on the home, but both share this clever mix, an offbeat touch and a taste for quirky original furniture; perhaps a prima donna's dressing table found in a hairdressing salon or a cheerfully tacky Formica cocktail bar.

€€

8 rue Bochart de Saron, 75009
06 74 58 11 91
www.dank.fr
Tue-Sat 13:00-19:30
M° Anvers

DANK

"The true moderns in the history of the 20th century were the Danish," believes François-Xavier Dousset, who is gently rubbing oil into a wooden dining chair in his small Pigalle gallery-cum-workshop; not the elitist international architect-designers, but the design of a tiny country, which produced an incredible amount of the furniture that actually found its way into people's living rooms all over the world. There's stuff from the 50s to 70s here, with some Artemide and other Italian lighting among the Scandinavians, but his real favourite is what he calls "the highpoint of Danish design" from 1955 to 1960, the period, he explains,

when you find the best richly coloured teak, clean lines and timeless forms, from small, semi-artisanal companies like Søborg Møbelfabrik or the FDB cooperative. François-Xavier will also happily introduce you to designers like Børge Mogensen and Peter Hvidt and Olga Mølgaard-Nielsen. He finds some items in France, but also frequently heads off to Denmark in search of furniture, which he gently cleans but is careful not to over-restore. En route he picks up some unusual German art pottery (also in the shop). DANK? Somewhere between Denmark and thank you.

€

ET PUIS C'EST TOUT

72 rue des Martyrs, 75009
01 40 23 94 02
Mon 14:00-19:00; Tue-Sat 12:00-19:30
M° Pigalle

This *brocanteur* is a fan of advertising
memorabilia and merchandising
souvenirs. Amid some Formica furniture
and odds and ends, pride of place goes
to an impressive variety of yellow Ricard
jugs and unusual commemorative clocks
evoking the timeless, pastis-drinking
France populaire. Gauloise ashtrays, Air
France plates, bar glasses and carafes
continue the theme, along with old
advertising posters and a crateful of
kitsch key rings.

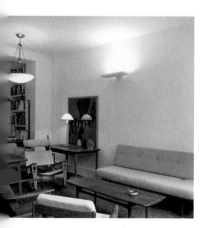

€€€

GALERIE CHRISTINE DIEGONI

47ter rue Orsel, 75018
01 42 64 69 48
www.christinediegoni.fr
Tue-Fri 14:00-19:00; Sat 11:00-19:00
M° Abbesses or Pigalle

Diegoni is a specialist, a rigorous devotee
of modern design and the acknowledged
expert on lighting by Italian designer
Gino Sarfatti, although she lets some
furniture by George Nelson and colourful
postmodern creations by Ettore Sottsass
creep in too.

€

MADAME CHOSE

94 rue Nollet, 75017
06 87 11 76 86
www.madamechose.fr
Wed-Sat 11:00-19:30
M° Brochant

At this recently opened vintage
decoration shop on a Batignolles side
street, Mélanie, alias 'Madame Thing',
keeps her prices low and choice personal,
with a shabby-chic edge to the miscellany
of old desks and school maps, lamps, small
bookcases, boomerang mirrors, pharmacy
boxes and multiple alarm clocks, picked
up from all over France. It's the sort of
place where you rediscover forgotten fads,
like the 70s craze for bamboo furniture.

BATIGNOLLES BITES

*a casual
boho bistro*

LES PUCES DES BATIGNOLLES

110 rue Legendre, 75017
01 42 26 62 26

Not a flea market but a casual boho
bistro furnished with vintage radios,
old industrial lighting and other flea
market finds. Packed and buzzy at
lunchtime for its good value daily
lunch menu, serving French bistro
classics with some inventive twists.

€€

MOBILHOME

106 rue Legendre, 75017
01 58 59 10 01
www.chezmobilhome.com
Tue-Sat 11:00-19:30
M° La Fourche

In a glass-fronted shop up in the
burgeoning Batignolles district,
Mobilhome has a good eye for the sort
of vintage that actually makes up a
home, wisely specialising in the type
of small everyday furniture, such as
neat bookcases or display cabinets, and
wood and metal desks, that can fit into
today's small Parisian flats. The emphasis
is on 50s to 70s, going for items that
have distinct vintage charm – think
coloured Formica panels, metal legs and
boomerang forms. Furniture is restored,
sometimes customised, and interspersed
in the shop with a line of new spidery
Mouille-inspired lamps and
clockwork robots.

€

L'OBJET QUI PARLE

86 rue des Martyrs, 75018
06 09 67 05 30
Mon-Sat 13:00-19:00
M° Abbesses

These 'objects that speak to you' have the
eclectic appeal and personal eccentricity
of an old-fashioned cabinet of curiosities,
piled together in a deliciously illogical
mix. Taking up every inch of the shop
and even overflowing onto the pavement
outside, this is a place for magpies, as
religious statues are posed amid enamel
coffee pots, stuffed birds, a stack of animal
antlers, old roadworks lamps and glass
chandeliers; anatomical models and
reptile skeletons reside next to perfectly
usable dinner services.

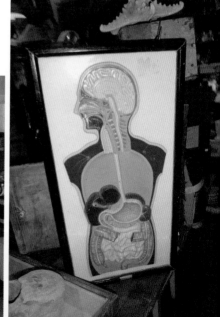

Spree/Papiers Peints

€€€

16 rue La Vieuville, 75018
01 42 23 41 40
www.spree.fr
Mon/Sun 15:00-19:00; Tue-Sat 11:00-19:00
M° Abbesses

Fashion stylist Roberta Oprandi and her artist-designer husband, Bruno Hadjadj, have created a particularly Montmartre take on the concept store, somewhere between laidback fashion boutique and white box art gallery, but without the scary pretension of the hipper-than-thou. A wall painting by Hadjadj extends along one side of the store, while up-to-the-minute fashion and accessories from designers like Marc Jacobs, Helmut Lang, Golden Goose, Margiela 6 and Acne are draped over vintage tables and studio chairs from designers including Sarfati, Colombo, Paulin, Eames, Memphis and Finnish designer Tapiovaara.

Since opening the original shop in 2000, they've also spread into a former paint store across the road, still labelled *Papiers Peints*, where the focus is on 50s to 80s furniture and changing art and photography shows. Prices are high but Hadjadj seeks out rare pieces – an incredible five-sided table by Belgian designer Willy Van der Meeren, lesser-known Scandinavian designs or the Dutch descendants of De Stijl – and willingly tells you all about them.

TOMBÉES DU CAMION

€

17 rue Joseph-le-Maistre, 75018
09 81 21 62 80
www.tombeesducamion.com
Daily 13:00-20:00
M° Blanche or Place de Clichy

Charles Mas proudly salvages all those leftovers no one else wants, buying up entire old factory lots, ends of series and shop clearances. Button and beads, lab materials, toys, plastic dolls and crates full of dolls' heads, strings of 1970s plastic beads, 1920s penny whistles, old printed labels, alarm clocks or shaving brushes mix the useful and the useless, which he displays with an artist's eye in surreal combinations that have a strange logic all of their own.

Other locations
44/47 passage des Panoramas, 75002
Marché Vernaison (see p112), Puces de St-Ouen

ZUT! FRÉDÉRIC DANIEL ANTIQUITÉS

€€

9 rue Ravignan, 75018
01 42 59 69 68
www.antiquites-industrielles.com
Wed-Sat 11:00-19:00 (closed 13:00-16:00); and Sun morning
M° Abbesses

If you're after big, this is the place to come. Frédéric Daniel specialises in industrial recuperation, and he clearly has a thing about clocks, with a whole collection of old station, factory and church clocks, some of them over a metre wide. There's also industrial lighting and floodlights, and even some unusual RATP tramway signals, as well as smaller items like desk lamps, office chairs, globes, stuffed animals and curios, or the cast-iron and wood Singer factory chairs and stools originally made for sewing factories.

€

ALASINGLINLIN

1 rue du Marché Popincourt, 75011
01 43 38 45 54
http://alasinglinglin.com
Tue-Fri 12:00-19:00; Sat/Sun 14:00-19:00
M° Oberkampf

Amid the cluster of *brocantes* and old
workshops in a tranquil backwater of
little streets just off heaving Oberkampf,
Alasinglinglin has a particularly good
selection of 50s and 60s furniture,
astuciously laid out as if round a room,
and a friendly welcome from the trio
of owners Natalie, Philippe and Bruno.
An unusual Z-bend coat stand, Formica
kitchen tables and chairs, some very
orange 50s armchairs, steel and wood
desks and a long wooden Scandinavian
sideboard catch the eye, with mainly
anonymous manufacturers joined by the
occasional well-known name (a Jacques
Adnet coffee table, a Bertoia diamond
chair). You'll also find some old school
science posters and metal advertising
plaques; and, yes, that really is a bicycle
hanging from the ceiling.

€€

ATELIER BULLE

8-10 passage Bullourde, 75011
01 58 30 96 37
http://bullelesite.free.fr
Wed-Sat 11:00-19:00 (or by appointment)
M° Ledru-Rollin

Marie and Audrey keep up the Faubourg
St-Antoine furniture-making tradition,
sort of; or rather they create new pieces
out of old 1950s and 60s furniture,
cheerfully reorganised and repainted
in sludge greys and bright colours in
their *atelier-boutique* where they also
organise occasional art shows or sales
by different creators.

ANNA COLORE INDUSTRIALE

€€

7 rue Paul-Bert, 75011
01 43 79 41 62
www.anna-colore-industriale.com
Wed-Fri 13:00-20:00; Sat 14:00-20:00
M° Faidherbe-Chaligny

Dressed in work overalls Anna Farina hauls a reconditioned black-metal printer's desk out of her van, shifting around some of the tables, industrial storage cabinets and stacks of metal chairs to squeeze it into her showroom-cum-workshop. *Colore* is not her surname, more like her motto: 'Anna colours'. She gives recuperated industrial furniture back its colours (preferably red); restoring, stripping back and repainting – "I like going back to the patinas underneath the varnish," she explains – and sometimes creates new assemblages, like an articulated metal desk lamp welded onto a jerry can. After careers as a scenographer, interior designer

and furniture designer, Italian Anna opened her shop in 2008 to satisfy a passion for metal furniture, with a taste for raw industrial looks. She eschews any mechanical sanding in favour of hand-finished cleaning and polishing, and redoes the colour/patina based on the original colour – "that respects its original colour and valorises its age and history." Some pieces are left almost untouched, while for more banal or damaged articles, she'll have fun giving them a new life with fresh colours and her own artistic touches. There's also a good selection of children's furniture, industrial lettering, piles of old factory lampshades and assorted storage tins and boxes.

€

BELLE LURETTE

5 rue du Marché Popincourt
01 43 38 67 39
www.villagepopincourt.com
Tue-Fri 12:00-19:00; Sat/Sun 14:00-19:00
M° Oberkampf

A large, cluttered *brocante dépôt-vente* with a wide variety of stuff, where hefty 19th century wardrobes and gilt mirrors mix with 20th century kitchen dressers, dinner services and eclectic lights. Less focused than the other Popincourt *brocantes*, but the sort of place where a sift can be worthwhile.

€

CAROUCHE

18 rue Jean-Macé, 75011
01 43 73 53 03
www.carouche.typepad.com
Tue-Sat 11:00-19:00 (closed Aug)
M° Charonne or Faidherbe-Chaligny

Industrial meets rustic at this charming small *brocante*. Caroline describes herself as an "interpreter of objects," picking up old chairs, industrial lighting, desks and storage cabinets, rusty iron garden seats, galvanised steel boxes and enamelled signs at *brocantes* and industrial sales, with the emphasis on character rather than design. Many of the pieces are reinterpreted – whether that means a simple paint job or recombination – and accessorized with glass cloches and cake stands, and some unclassifiable oddities – pink metal wire flamingos (what on earth were they for?) or a stuffed parrot.

€

LE CHÂTEAU DE MA MÈRE

108 avenue Ledru-Rollin, 75011
01 43 14 26 03
Tue-Sat 11:30-19:30
M° Ledru-Rollin

A *brocante* for babies, with a cheerful clutter of soft toys, building bricks, high chairs, painted wardrobes and toy chests, toddler-sized armchairs and plenty of baby clothes too.

€€

COIN CANAL

1 rue de Marseille, 75010
01 42 38 00 30
www.coincanal.net
Tue-Fri 11:00-19:30 (closed 14:00-15:00);
Sat 11:00-19:30
M° Jacques Bonsergent

Located up amid a growing fashion selection near the Canal St-Martin, this smart corner shop specialises in mid-century Scandinavian design: angular sofas, armchairs (lots of orange), sideboards and teak dining tables, imposing desks and modular shelving systems. Everything is in excellent condition, though somewhat snooty and expensive to go with it.

€€

COLONEL

14 avenue Richerand, 75010
01 83 89 69 22
www.moncolonelvintage.fr
Tue-Sat 10:00-19:00
M° Jacques Bonsergent

Colonel got its name from one of those old-fashioned lime and vermouth long drinks and it suits the summery retro appeal of the showroom, where the designer duo Colonel, alias Isabelle Gilles and Yann Poncelet, present their own retro-inspired lamp and chair designs, handmade by craftsmen in the French provinces, and the vintage pieces that Poncelet has unearthed at flea markets. It's mainly timeless Scandinavian design, such as wooden craft dining chairs painted in cheerful colours, Danish armchairs and low tables, set off by a scattering of Turkish rugs, Moroccan baskets and batik cushions.

€€

COMPLÉMENT D'OBJET

11 rue Jean-Pierre Timbaud, 75011
01 43 57 09 28/06 09 16 55 81
www.complementdobjet.com
Wed-Sat 15:30-20:00
M° République or Oberkampf

Here's it's all about lighting as the essential complement to an interior. Patrice Rotenstein has filled his shop with so many lamps you can hardly get in; it's like a quick whiz through lighting styles of the past 80 years. All jumbled together are art deco table lamps and 1990s chrome, 70s ceramic, a 50s Rispal 'praying mantis' and Reggiani wooden totem, Italian desk lamps, or aluminium suspensions and assorted versions of the articulated metal Gras lamp (French equivalent of the Anglepoise). More lamps and iron lanterns dangle from the ceiling in the cellar. It's inspiring and unsorted for all tastes, designer and deco, with Rotenstein happy to fish lamps out of the depths.

GALERIE PATRICK SEGUIN

€€€

5 rue des Taillandiers, 75011
01 40 21 82 95
www.patrickseguin.com
Mon-Sat 10:00-19:00
M° Bastille

Patrick Seguin has become virtually synonymous with Jean Prouvé, being one of the first to resurrect the designer's reputation and to collect not only Prouvé's avant-garde industrial furniture, often made for student residences, but also to buy up his experimental prefabricated architecture and even fragments of his now cult modular architectural systems. Today, Prouvé's pieces are the preserve of millionaires and museums, but Seguin's well-documented shows are well worth a visit, sometimes even displaying entire constructions, such as the Maison Metropole, a demountable housing unit, and the Maison des jours meilleurs (home for better days), prototype accommodation for the homeless that sadly never saw the light of day. A few other architect-designers get featured too, notably Charlotte Perriand and Le Corbusier, and the airy gallery itself was designed by Jean Nouvel.

PUDDING

€

24 rue du Marché Popincourt, 75011
06 80 36 95 59
www.villagepopincourt.com
Wed-Fri 12:00-19:00; Sat/Sun 14:00-19:00
M° Oberkampf

An authentic secondhand clutter among the easygoing Popincourt *brocantes*, where you might find old school maps, witches' mirrors, leather club chairs or weighty desks, cupboards and lamps, assorted paintings and family photos.

€

RECYCLING

3 rue Neuve Popincourt, 75011
01 43 57 48 40
www.brocanterecycling.fr
Tue-Fri 12:00-19:00; Sat/Sun 14:00-21:00
M° Oberkampf

An *atelier-brocante* with an ecological
edge, where Dominique Archambault
takes a light-hearted approach to
recuperation with an atmospheric, eclectic
selection of painted 1950s wood and zinc
kitchen dressers, old industrial lighting,
repainted first aid cabinets, champagne
glasses and giant metal letters. As an
intriguing sideline she makes an oddball
range of cushions (made from old fabric)
and hundreds of hand-stitched cotton
'Cling Cling' rabbits with barmy slogans
("Cling Cling says out loud what you say
in your head").

OBERKAMPF BITES

*real Italian
pizza by
the slice*

AL TAGLIO

2 bis rue Neuve Popincourt, 75011
01 43 38 12 00

Across the street from Recyling, real
Italian pizza by the slice is sold by
the kilo, to eat around convivial, high
communal wooden tables or to take away.
It's streaks above the competition, with
a choice between classics and inventive
daily variations.

€

AUX CÉRISES DE LUTÈCE

86 rue Monge, 75005
01 43 31 67 51
Mon-Sat 11:00-17:30
M° Place Monge

A sign of the gentrification of the Latin Quarter is the ever-increasing number of tea shops, but this one is old-school bohemian: a tea room-cum-*brocante*, where along with tea and cakes in the afternoon or salads and quiches at lunch, you can buy the bric-a-brac on the shelves, the jewellery, the chair you are sitting on or the cup you're drinking from.

€€

DANS L'AIR DU TEMPS

12 rue Lacépède, 75005
01 42 17 06 39
Tue-Sat 14:30-19:00 (closed Aug)
M° Place Monge

The line of jugs in the window immediately catches the eye here, and although there is some vintage furniture – wrought-iron lamps, spiky chandeliers, drinks trolleys, magazine racks – it's particularly good for ceramics. Owner Denise Achard is totally dedicated to the 1950s and although she says it's getting harder and harder to find good pieces, she still comes up with an impressive range and reasonable prices, notably numerous jugs and vases, flamboyantly painted bowls and Luc's bicolour forms from Vallauris' 1950s heyday.

€

LILAS PORT ROYAL

72 boulevard du Port Royal, 75005
01 43 31 65 09
www.lilasdecoration.com
Mon-Sat 09:00-19:00
RER Port-Royal

Just the sort of old-fashioned, unpretentious neighbourhood *brocante* you need, Lilas buys mainly from individuals and does a lot of house clearances so there are all genres and all periods. There are occasional bargains to be found, with anything from a Gae Aulenti lamp or art deco clock to a full-scale cast-iron fountain amid the mahogany dressers, garden chairs, Limoges dinner services, Thonet dining chairs and discarded sculptures and paintings.

LUMIÈRE D'OEIL

An extraordinary shop which makes you yearn for the flickering days of gaslight.

€€

4 rue Flatters, 75005
01 47 07 63 47
http://lumiara.perso.neuf.fr/lumiara/en
Tue-Fri 14:00-19:00; Sat 11:00-17:00
M° Gobelins or RER Port-Royal

Monsieur Ara comes in a category all of his own, because while other people covet antique lamps for their design and structure, their beautiful bronze or glass, what really fascinates Monsieur Ara is how they work: the chemical reaction, the right fuel, correct wick and perfect shade to create the best flame and light.

Although a few early electric examples do get in (and he can adapt gas lamps for electrical use, while being careful not to damage the original mechanism), the real treasure trove is the shelves laden with antique oil, paraffin and spirit lamps, from the late 18th to the early 20th centuries, in a whole wealth of decorative styles and materials, as Monsieur Ara initiates you into the different techniques and manufacturers.

Behind the shop proper is Monsieur Ara's workshop and personal museum, where he proudly shows me his own collection of lighting history and lights an ingenious brass gas lamp he has just acquired. Born in Turkey in an Armenian family, he arrived in France by way of Germany, and studies in chemistry, and tells me he is able to give guided visits of his collection in five languages. An extraordinary shop, which makes you yearn for the flickering days of gaslight as he picks out a lamp in Birmingham opaline glass, lamps in marble or porcelain and even a primitive radiator.

€€

LE CUBE ROUGE

11 rue Lalande, 75014
06 11 60 30 03
www.lecuberouge.com
Open Tue/Thu/Fri 13:00-19:30; Sat 10:30-
19:30; Sun 10:30-13:30
M° Denfert-Rochereau

This tiny cube of a shop just off the rue
Daguerre market street is a favourite
with local architects, with 1950s and
60s furniture – by all sorts of designers
including George Nelson, Arne Jacobsen,
Pierre Paulin and Hans Bellman , as well
as unknowns but always with an eye for
quality – for sale and hire.

€€

ESPACES 54

54 rue Mazarine, 75006
09 51 36 18 48
www.espaces54.com
Tue-Sat 14:00-19:00
M° Mabillon or Odéon

"Even if it's beautiful and vintage, it has
to be something practical that one needs,"
believes Juliette Aittouares-Caillon, who
creates a whole apartment look rather
than a gallery feel, subscribing to the idea
of "furniture to live with." Pieces from the
50s to 70s by the big international names
such as Eames, Van der Rohe, Panton and
Loewy – and others who merit discovery,
like Pierre Guariche or Willy Van der
Meeren – are complemented by
artists' carpets and occasional
photography shows.

€€€

GALERIE DOWNTOWN

18 and 33 rue de Seine, 75006
01 46 33 82 41
www.galeriedowntown.com
Tue-Sat 10:30-19:00 (closed 13:00-14:00)
M° Mabillon or St-Germain-des-Prés

Rue de Seine, at the heart of St-Germain gallery land, has become a treasure trove for sought-after modern design classics, and François Laffanour was the first to move in here in 1980, showcasing design from the 1940s and 50s by avant-garde architects and designers. On one side of the street, it's mainly classics like a Prouvé desk or Serge Mouille's spider-like black metal lamps; across the street it's more contemporary editions and one-off pieces by today's designers like Ron Arad, Gaetano Pesce and Byung Hoon Choi.

€€€

GALERIE MATTHIEU RICHARD

34 rue de Seine, 75006
01 56 24 44 87
www.matthieurichard.fr
Tue-Sat 10:30-19:00 (closed 12:30-14:00)
M° Mabillon or St-Germain-des-Prés

Sophie and Matthieu Richard specialise in the distinctive pierced sheet metal furniture and lamps created by Mathieu Matégot in the 1950s, which is functional with a touch of fantasy, in inventive forms, and with curvaceous flourishes. You'll also find some pieces by Jean Prouvé and Charlotte Perriand or elegant 40s and 50s Jacques Adnet and Jean Royére.

€€€

GALERIE JACQUES LACOSTE

12 rue de Seine, 75006
01 40 20 41 82
Tue-Sat 11:00-19:00 (closed 13:00-14:00)
M° Mabillon or St-Germain-des-Prés

Lacoste's predilection is for Jean Royère, a fashionable decorator who created interiors for a luxury clientele in the 1940s and 50s, though you'll also find the wood sculptures and sculptural wooden bowls of Alexandre Noll, glass from Max Ingrand and some 20th century ceramics.

€€€

JOUSSE ENTREPRISE

18 rue de Seine, 75006
01 53 82 13 60
www.jousse-entreprise.com
Mon 14:00-19:00; Tue-Sat 11:00-19:00
M° Mabillon

Philippe Jousse started out with a stall at St-Ouen flea market (see p110) before opening his first art gallery in the Bastille with Patrick Seguin (see p95), and he's kept up the dual interest ever since. It's contemporary art at his gallery in the 13th arrondissement, and modern design classics here, where you might find furniture by Jean Prouvé or sections of Prouvé's innovative prefabricated buildings, alongside Serge Mouille lamps, the elegant monochrome vases of ceramicist Georges Jouve, and work by the more recent designers of the 70s and 80s, like Pierre Paulin, who decorated the Élysée Palace for President Pompidou, or Roger Tallon, designer of the first TGV. Philippe's favourite, perhaps, are the monochrome pebble vases and elegant minimalist forms of ceramicist Georges Jouve, which are posed delicately around the gallery.

ST-GERMAIN BITES

The original artists' café, with its Art Nouveau woodwork, palettes over the bar and paintings on the walls

LA PALETTE

43 rue de Seine, 75006
01 43 26 68 15

The original artists' café, with its Art Nouveau woodwork, palettes over the bar and paintings on the walls, supposedly donated by impoverished artists, and an excellent people-watching terrace. A relaxed place for a drink, steak tartare or croque monsieur.

AGAPÉ SUBSTANCE

66 rue Mazarine, 75006
01 43 29 33 83
www.agapesubstance.com

An eatery for modern design collectors; it's experimental gourmet cooking with lots of tiny tasting dishes and mysterious herbs, served down a long communal table in a white, gallery-like space.

€ €
LE PASSÉ D'AUJOURD'HUI

43 rue du Cherche-Midi, 75006
01 42 22 41 21
Mon 15:00-19:00; Tue-Sat 10:00-19:00
(closed 14:00-15:00)
Mᵒ Sèvres-Babylone

It's hard to know whether Le Passé d'Aujourd'hui fits into the fashion or antiques bracket, because its passion is clearly art deco as a style that spans the arts. In furniture you might find a gleaming walnut veneer and tubular steel desk, cubic bedside cabinets, decorative items like vases, wine glasses and lamps, and elegant croco handbags; while the fashion element includes a selection of jewellery that goes from simple geometric Bakelite bracelets and dog brooches to a Schiaparelli extravaganza, with appropriately eclectic pricing to match.

€

LA SALLE DES VENTES DU PARTICULIER

117 rue d'Alesia, 75014
01 45 42 42 42
www.lasalledesventes.fr
Daily 10:00-19:00
M° Alésia

This vast warehouse-style furniture *dépôt vente* spread over two storeys is a Parisian institution, with a vast range of goods going from inexpensive sets of dining chairs, rustic wardrobes and old sofas (even an entire 1960s kitchen on a recent visit) to period secretaire desks and tables – and a godsend to anyone looking to rapidly furnish a flat. You might find Napoléon III furniture, pairs of leather club chairs, perhaps an art deco dressing table, modern lamps, portrait busts and animalier bronzes, a 50s washing machine, antique coal scuttles or an imposing ceramic stove. Sellers set their own prices, which come down gradually if items remain unsold. It's buyer beware, as repro mixes with genuine antiques, but there are real bargains to be had, with prices often much lower than at the *puces* or in the design shops. Act fast if you see something you like, as good finds tend to get snapped up quickly.

Other location
63 quai de Seine, 75019

€€

SERENDIPITY

81-83 rue du Cherche-Midi, 75006
01 42 22 12 18
www.serendipity.fr
Tue-Sat 11:00-19:00
M° Sèvres-Babylone

A stylish concept store for kids in a
beautiful and airy converted garage,
with furniture and design and all sorts
of adorable toys, gadgets and bathroom
goodies that are far too desirable to give
to a child. Although the stock is mainly
new, there's also a covetable selection
of vintage, with restored and repainted
desks, wardrobes and cradles.

€€€

VELVET GALERIE

11 rue Guénégaud, 75006
01 43 26 14 90
www.velvet-galerie.com
Tue-Sat 14:00-19:00
M° St-Germain-des-Prés

If classic modern design all seems a little
too sober and functional, then Velvet goes
for the fantastical end of the 60s and 70s; a
world where design means vinyl, Plexiglas
and fibreglass and forms often look closer
to sci-fi than interior design. Gallerist
Benoît Ramognino has a particular
mission to rehabilitate forgotten
landmarks like the inflatable furniture
of Quasar Khanh and the almost fungal
organic forms of Jean-Pierre Laporte
(intriguingly, one of his chairs, the *girolle*,
is even named after a type of mushroom),
or the Utopian space-capsule architectural
prototypes of Matti Suuronen and work of
German designer Luigi Colani. The goods
are shown in a delirious environment of
pop art and shaggy carpets.

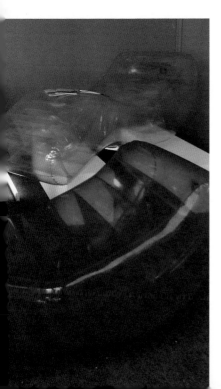

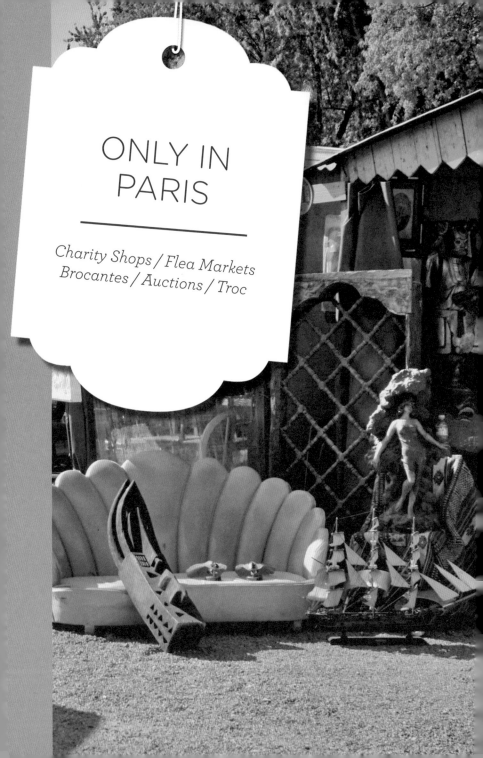

ONLY IN PARIS

Charity Shops / Flea Markets
Brocantes / Auctions / Troc

THERE'S A PROFUSION OF YESTERDAYS IN THE CACOPHONY OF DROUOT, HUB OF THE PARIS AUCTION SYSTEM, OR THE MARCHÉ AUX PUCES DE SAINT-OUEN, THE LARGEST FLEA MARKET IN THE WORLD, COMPLEMENTED BY A YEAR-LONG CALENDAR OF *BROCANTES* AND FAIRS THAT GOES FROM ATTIC CLEAR-OUTS TO SERIOUS ANTIQUES MARKETS. THESE PLACES GIVE A UNIQUE VISION OF THE PARISIAN LIFESTYLE, THE PLACES FOR WEEKEND *CHINEURS*, EVER-HOPEFUL BARGAIN-HUNTERS AND A MARKET SPIRIT OF BANTER AND BARGAINING.

THE FLEA MARKETS

The Paris flea markets grew up in the late 19th century when the *chiffoniers* (rag merchants) and *ferrailleurs* (scrap metal dealers) set up on what was originally undevelopable land in the shadow of the city walls, so they didn't have to pay tax duties on bringing goods into the city. The dealers sold their – often flea-ridden, hence the name – wares to Parisians who came out at weekends for a Sunday promenade or to enjoy the *guinguette* dance halls of what were then semi-rural surrounding villages. Apart from the tiny market at place d'Aligre, the flea markets are still located on the edge of Paris *intra-muros* (as the cluster of 20 Paris arrondissements is known), and even at highly organised, often upmarket St-Ouen there's still a seedy section where the *biffins* (slang for *chiffonier*), who scavenge junk from dustbins, spread out their finds on the pavement.

PUCES DE SAINT-OUEN (CLIGNANCOURT)

Rue des Rosiers, rue Paul-Bert and rue Jules-Vallès, 93400 Saint-Ouen
www.marcheauxpuces-saintouen.com
Sat-Mon 09:30-18:00
M° Porte de Clignancourt

Inspiration for countless fashion designers in search of new ideas or reels of old lace, or American decorators after the French château look, St-Ouen could be called the Louvre of flea markets – and that's not the trite comparison it might seem. The flea market consists of over two thousand stalls, spread over some 15 individual markets, most of them running off rue des Rosiers, each with its different character, and, like the Louvre, you can come back again and again, think you know every gallery and yet still discover a small alleyway, a stand or an extraordinary object you didn't know before. There's also a continual renewal. Some stallholders have been here for 20 or 30 years, some stands are multi-generational family affairs, others have just arrived, succumbing to the temptation of having their own stall – the rest of the week to *chine*, to haunt the auction houses, research and restore. It's a sign of the times, and the craze for vintage, that even design store Habitat is opening its own vintage outlet, Habitat 1964, on rue des Rosiers, where it will buy and sell its own products from the 1960s to 90s.

You can see why André Breton, Max Ernst, Salvador Dali and other Surrealist writers and artists were so fascinated by the Marché aux Puces in the 1920s and 30s, with its piling up of epochs and cultures, strange juxtapositions, source of ready-made found objects, composite Surrealist objects or 'culture rearranged'. André Breton describes the appeal of St-Ouen in *Nadja*: "I am often there, in search of those objects that one finds nowhere else, outdated, broken, unusable, almost incomprehensible, perverse even in the sense where I extend it and where I love it..." Breton had an indefatigable passion for amassing unusual objects – tribal and folk art, shells, drawings, sculptures, Eskimo masks, pre-Columbian statues, holy water stoups, books, photos and generally strange objects that fascinated him and gradually filled his apartment in 42 rue Fontaine in Pigalle, one wall of it now conserved at the Centre Pompidou.

If you're coming from Porte de Clignancourt metro station, persevere until you have gone underneath the Périphérique ring road to the suburb of St-Ouen, to rue de Rosiers and the flea market proper. On your way you will be assailed by touts brandishing fake Louis Vuitton bags and Burberry check purses, followed by a drag of cheap clothing stalls out there to trap tourists who do not realise that the real market is still to come.

Part of the fun of the *puces* is that you really can still find everything or anything here at prices that go from a few centimes to several thousand euros. It is the sort of place where you come looking for a teapot and leave carrying a coat rack or a necklace. The *puces* is a mini city in itself, complete with plenty of cafés and places to eat (see p124), shippers to take goods home, a branch of the St-Ouen tourist office, and a lifestyle all of its own, so much so that the whole area has been heritage listed for its unique atmosphere.

If you can, pay several visits to get a feel of which markets interest you most, the sort of goods available and the range of prices to expect. A little bargaining is part of the game – Saint-Ouen likes to keep up its market image, after all – but this is not a souk, items here all have marked prices and you shouldn't expect to get much more than 10 percent or, rarely, 20 percent off, or perhaps a discount if you buy several items. Mondays are quieter than weekends but there are also fewer stalls open, while some of the markets also open on Thursday and Friday mornings for professionals only.

The seven market guides that follow here, from Marché Vernaison through to Marché Jules Valles, all fall within the Puces de Saint-Ouen complex. Paris' other flea markets are covered from p125 onwards.

MARCHÉ VERNAISON

AT PUCES DE SAINT-OUEN
99 rue des Rosiers/136 avenue Michelet
www.vernaison.net

The oldest of the St-Ouen markets opened in 1918 when Romain Jules Vernaison put up the first shacks for *brocanteurs* and it's still the one that stays closest to the true flea market spirit with a tangle of narrow alleyways and wildly eclectic stands. This is a place where you can still find bargains, but what is truly wonderful is the sheer eclecticism – as you wander between organised shops with glazed vitrines and shambolic stands – from piles of unknowns and bric-a-brac, generalists mixing furniture, ceramics and lamps to

specialists, perhaps in ceramics, fashion accessories, posters or glass, who are incredibly knowledgeable and willing to show off and explain their treasures. With over 250 stalls, its fan-shaped layout and assorted entrances off rue des Rosiers and avenue Michelet, it's impossible to be systematic; more the sort of market where you just have to keep exploring.

'Future is Vintage' proclaims the writing on the window at **David Roy** (allée 1, stand 3), a haute couture feast, where Edwige David-Roy guides regular clients and Russian tourists through her prize items, with a whole rail of Chanel tweed jackets, and designer evening gowns from the likes of Dior, amid paintings and animalier ceramics and objets d'art.

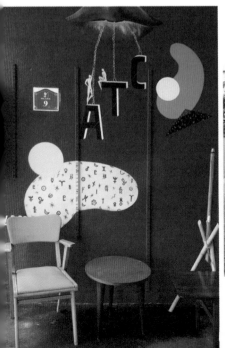

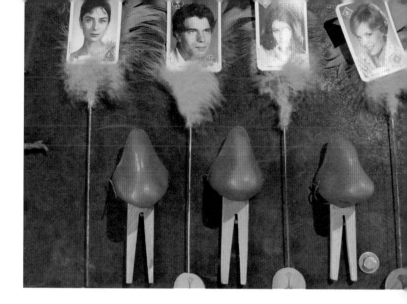

At **Au Temps Conté** (allée 1, stand 15) Corinne specialises in 1950s to 70s design, with an eye for quirky metal lights and Scandinavian sideboards and dining tables. At **Au Grenier de Lucie** (allée 1, stand 25), former schoolteachers Jason and Heidi Ellis have a striking array of jewellery from fashion houses Yves Saint Laurent and Chanel, colourful, sparkly creations by American Miriam Haskell, graphic 1970s Bakelite by Guillemette L'Hoir, as well as an unusual sideline in bejewelled crowns made for religious statues.

There's a feast of cheerful vintage Americana at **The Duke** (allée 1, stand 37) – think baseball jackets and chrome and leatherette bars and bar stools – while **Galerie Paul Maurel** (allée 1, stand 41; www.poster-paul.com) is an institution for vintage posters, advertising prints and old copies of *Elle* and *Paris Match*, perhaps with BB on the cover. At **Les Deux Ourses** (allée 5, stand 84) seek out vintage clothes and accessories, notably lots of smart croco bags.

At **Tombées du Camion** (allée 7, stand 126/allée 3, stand 107a) – the name means 'fell off the back of a lorry' – the speciality is complete job lots of dolls' heads and arms, shaving brushes, buttons and other miscellanea, although the real appeal is the way they are arranged into fantastical composite collages on the walls.

There's old lace and embroidery at **Francine Dentelles** (allée 7, stands 121-123, 132; www.francine-dentelles.com), ranging from delicate antique wedding dresses to baby wear, embroidered shawls and samplers, beadwork bags and household linen; and fountain pens and writing implements at **Boulevard des Ecritures** (allée 7, stand 128), with lots of Chanel bags and jewellery at **Aux Trésors de Babeth** (allée 7, stand 140).

Wonderwir (allée 7, stand 146bis) is the sort of place that cheers you up in the sometimes over-serious collecting scene with a wonderful array of kitsch and curios, such as old snowstorms, 50s metal lamps and Vallauris lustre ceramic shell and fish lamps, toys and costume jewellery. There's a more upmarket selection of jewellery at **Eva** (allée 7, stand 153), with beautiful art deco necklaces and silver bracelets, which the proprietor will happily let you try on, and boudoir accessories. After jewellery in glass cases, **Christian de Corbiac**'s shop (allée 7, stand 154bis) is a cheerful cacophony with so many plates, vases and tankards piled on the floor you can hardly get in. With a mix of china, glassware, pewter, oil paintings, cutlery and wooden crucifixes, it's great if you're after a vase or aristocratic serving dish and he'll happily wade through the items to fish out what has caught your eye.

Denise Balbon (allée 8, stand 185) has been specialising in antique glass for over 25 years, and was an expert for Christie's and, later, Drouot before setting up here. Most of her glass is 19th century, with a few earlier pieces, and most is from Bohemia and the Lorraine. "The most knowledgeable collectors are German and English," she says, showing off rare tumblers with the signs of the horoscope and wine glasses engraved with hunting scenes originally made for a château in the Loire. Or there's **Laetitia Georges** (allée 8, stand 192bis; www.fandeventails. com), a fan specialist with a huge variety of pieces on sale, from delicate hand-painted 18th century fans to novelty and advertising fans, and 19th century lace fans. **Torbati Antiquité** (allée 8, stand 196/allée 9, stand 224) is good for period furniture including fine antique carved gilt mirrors, marquetry cabinets and sécretaire desks. Among several toy stalls, **La Farandole** (allée 9, stand 912) attracts serious collectors with a 'farandole' (a lively Provençal dance) of melancholy Steiff teddy bears, antique china dolls, dolls' teasets and furniture, dolls' clothes and even dolls' wigs.

MARCHÉ BIRON

AT PUCES DE SAINT-OUEN
85 rue des Rosiers
www.marchebiron.fr

With its two long alleys, Biron was the first market in the *puces* to have fixed boutiques when it opened in 1925, sign from the start that it was a more upmarket affair than Vernaison. Traditional and tranquil, Allée 1 is awash in gilt mirrors, ormolu furniture and crystal chandeliers for furnishing period apartments but also has quality collectors' finds with posters, Lalique glass, 1950s furniture and objets d'art. At **Le Curieux** (stand 126) fan specialist Serge Davoudian has delicate fans and shagreen nécessaire sets. At **Casa Bella** (stands 94-95, 70), it's the ceramics that catch the eye as Hélène Cabarrouy shows off Jean Cocteau plates, and sculptural yellow and black jugs, china eggs and other art pottery by Pol Chambost.

The second alley concentrates more on period woodwork and furniture, being a good source of big old office desks that seem to linger from some obscure civil service office, mahogany bookcases and dining tables, fireplaces, drawing boards, telegram desks and spiral library stairs.

MARCHÉ PAUL BERT

AT PUCES DE SAINT-OUEN
96 rue des Rosiers/18 rue Paul Bert
www.paulbert-serpette.com

An outdoor market with booths stretching around and behind the Marché Serpette (see p121), this is many people's favourite market, with its on the ball, convivial feel, an excellent café and bright outdoor setting. It also reflects the changing trends of collecting and interior decoration. The first to see dealers specialising in 50s to 70s design, with just a few stands 20 years ago, the market now has more and more specialists in vintage items, from 50s metal lamps and chairs to cult items of 80s furniture, so take time to sift through the choice.

Maxbox Design (allée 1, stand 61; www. maxboxdesign.com) is a good source of metal Bertoia chairs and covetable 50s coatstands, or 60s ceramics and kinetic metal lampshades. **Fatmir Taraj** (allée 1, stand 19) has a choice of the classic Knoll pedestal dining table designed by Eero Saarinen in 1956 (and still in production), not only in the familiar white but also in the rarer streaky green and black marble versions. **AJ'tation**, alias Antoine Geoffroy d'Assy (allée 2, stand 131), is particularly good for Scandinavian sideboards and 70s lamps. **Flavien Gaillard** (allée 5, stand 202; www.flaviengaillard.com) is dedicated to the 60s of plastic flying-saucer lamps, flaky aluminium lights or Jean-Louis Avril's pieces in cardboard.

Dominique Ilous (allée 7, stands 409-411) was one of the pioneers in selling 20th century furniture 25 years ago, and has an excellent selection of 50s and 60s furniture and lighting, mainly by French and Italian designers. Nearby, **Thomas Tardif** (allée 7, stand 284) is a newcomer who strikes with his eye for pieces a little out of the ordinary – when I discovered him he had a 40s desk, an Ecole de Paris portrait, a recent Christophe Pillet daybed and two unusual 50s lamps depicting the *Fables de la Fontaine*.

There are plenty of other things at Paul Bert, too. **Bachelier Antiques** (allée 1, stand 17; www.bachelier-antiquites.com) is a cult address for cookery buffs. Its lovingly displayed antique kitchenwares

go from well-polished copper pans, terrines and utensils for nostalgics of old farmhouse kitchens, massive butchers' blocks and bottling apparatus right down to, literally, the antique kitchen sink. **Aux 3 Singes** (allée 1, stand 20; www.aux3singes. com) has a fabulous array of antique garden statuary and urns, essential for recreating the romantic lost *vie de château* look, from carved cherubs or stags at bay to giant reconstituted stone toadstools; while **Marc Maison** (allée 6, stand 83; www.marcmaison.fr; plus 120 rue des Rosiers for fireplaces) specialises in architectural salvage, in garden statuary, fireplaces and chimney pieces, panelling, iron railings, doors and gateposts. A pair of sphinxes for your garden? Or perhaps a quirky dog kennel c.1900?

MARCHÉ DAUPHINE

AT PUCES DE SAINT-OUEN
132/140 rue de Rosiers
www.marche-dauphine.com

This purpose built, two-storey market hall opened in 1991, yet still has a genuine 'pucey' feel with a wide variety of goods and prices. Among the dealers to look out for on the ground floor are **Leda Antiques** for its period gilt-framed mirrors and antique barometers, chandeliers and 18th century furniture; and Art et Cuirs (stands 35-38), a specialist in ornately decorated Napoleon III aperitif sets, often with boulle marquetry or mother-of-pearl inlay boxes and sets of glasses and decanters.

Michael Klein (stand 151) specialises in the *haute époque* – carved 16th century tables and Spanish cabinets, and carved wooden Baroque sculptures; while **Dezign +** (stand 253) resides firmly in a 20th century futurescape with Eero Aarnio's acrylic bubble chairs and child-sized Panton chairs from the golden age of plastic. Also on the ground floor, **Lucette and Nadine** (stand 78-79) is an Ali Baba's cavern of vintage evening wear, costume jewellery and elegant hats and bags. Then there's the fascination of **Daniel et Lili** (stand 128), under the *verrière*, pretty much in the middle of the market, where you can rummage through old buttons, wooden beads, reels of ribbon and lace, endless plastic combs, bead flowers, glass phials, vast old job lots of haberdashery and brooches, folios of old prints – sorted by subject from cows and cars to fashion – and vintage saucy postcards.

Upstairs, on the first floor, on one side you find extraordinary period clothing at the extensive stall of **Falbalas** (stands 284-285; http://falbalas.puces.free.fr/), much of it closer to historic costume than fashion, 19th century wasp-waisted dresses, colonial suits, boned corsets on dummies, and rails of 20s, 30s and 40s dresses arranged by decade. They also make their own line of period-inspired lace-up boots; and rent out costumes for film productions. On the other side is the **Carré des Libraires**, a cluster of secondhand booksellers, with stalls of books, prints, posters, 19th century photos and old postcards.

Passion Graphique at Marché Dauphine

Passion Graphique is aptly named for its wonderful selection of modernist transport posters. The proprietor, Laurent Noclain, studied art and worked as a poster restorer for collectors and poster specialists before opening his own stand at the end of 2011, and he still restores posters in his *atelier* in Tourcoing, near Lille. His favourites are the great transport posters of the 1920s and 30s, with their superb graphic style and typography by designers like Cassandre and Roger Broders that capture the whole aura of train travel and the Côte d'Azur, as well as later posters by Razzia, who continued the graphic tradition in the 1970s in posters for Vuitton or Roland Garros.

MARCHÉ SERPETTE

AT PUCES DE SAINT-OUEN
110 rue des Rosiers
www.marcheserpette.com

An upmarket quadrangle opened in the 1970s with carpeted aisles and booths in what was once a garage (it still has a useful car park on the roof), Serpette draws a smart international clientele with antique and costume jewellery, vintage clothes, statuary and antique furniture or entire walls of period panelling.

Look for glossy, highly polished art deco cocktail bars and display cabinets at **Ebony & Ivory** (allée 4, stand 16), old trunks and luggage, steamship memorabilia at **Le Monde de Voyage** (allée 3, stand 10) and 20th century design in modern carpets and Scandinavian sideboards at Julie Fortune (allée 1, stand 29bis). **Mezzanotte** (allée 6, stand 7) has art nouveau and art deco glass, while there are other dealers who'll mix everything from oil paintings, Napoleon III desks and icons to Baccarat glass and 60s furniture.

Artemise et Cunégonde (allée 1, stand 28; www.artemiseetcunegonde.com) is great for designer labels and fashion from the 1920s onwards, while British-born **Olwen Forest** (allée 3, stand 5; www.olwenforest.com) is an institution at Serpette with her *bijoux de stars*, an astonishing array of vintage and couture costume jewellery, including lots of Chanel, desirable early Schiaparelli, Joseff of Hollywood and Kenneth Jay Lane. High prices, but Olwen is extremely knowledgeable if you're looking for quality stuff with a cinematic touch.

MARCHÉ MALASSIS

AT PUCES DE SAINT-OUEN
85 rue des Rosiers

Another recent purpose-built arcade with a lot of glitz, shiny art deco and a reputation for (over)restored furniture that appeals more to decorators than experts. There are also carpet sellers, toys and bric-a-brac. Check out Chanel specialist **Mandara** (stand 71) for the quilted bag in umpteen versions, Chanel jackets and Vuitton luggage, or **Watch Deco** (stand 71) for watches including now cult 70s LIP models, and **La Collectionnite** (stand 5), a vintage toy stall.

MARCHÉ JULES VALLÈS

AT PUCES DE SAINT-OUEN
7-9 rue Jules Vallès

Some way out on its own along rue Jules Vallès, where you'll still find *biffins* spreading out their goods on blankets on the pavement, the Marché Jules Vallès is unashamedly shabby. In its two alleys, unlike Serpette or Biron, the stalls are piled up with largely unrestored items, drawing bargain hunters for lots of furniture, heaps of chairs, antique boat beds, gramophones, bronze statues or oddities like a collection of toy garages.

PUCES BITES

Pause at the puces for a bite

LE PAUL BERT

20 rue Paul Bert
01 40 11 90 28

A long narrow brasserie wedged into the corner of the Marché Paul Bert; a great place for brasserie standards and big salads, or simply for an afternoon drink at one of the outdoor tables.

CHEZ LOUISETTE

130 avenue Michelet (inside Marché Vernaison)
06 50 27 11 96

Touristy but fun *bistro-chansonnier* buried right inside Marché Vernaison (follow the signs when you're in the market). Perfect for *moules-frites* (mussels and chips), eaten to the accompaniment of singers belting out covers by Piaf etc.

PIZZERIA LE NAPOLI

136 rue des Rosiers
01 40 11 15 00

A genuine Italian bar and *ristorante* for classic pasta and pizza, Italian salads and *plats du jour*, all served by friendly staff.

LA CHOPE DES PUCES

122 rue des Rosiers
01 40 11 28 80

Jazz manouche, or gypsy jazz, is said to have been invented at the *puces* and this café-bistro keeps up the tradition, swinging to live music on weekend afternoons.

PUCES DE MONTREUIL

Avenue du Professeur André Lemierre, 75020
Sat/Sun/Mon 07:00-19:00
Mᵒ Porte de Montreuil

Should Montreuil even be called a flea market any more? It's hard to say. Occupying a long triangular strip next to the Périphérique ring road (if you're coming from Porte de Montreuil metro, cross place de la Porte de Montreuil and just follow the crowd), it's occupied more and more by stands of cheap clothes (jeans, synthetic dresses, socks and underwear), electrical parts and light bulbs, car paints and accessories, five-euro watches, trainers of dubious provenance and less and less genuine secondhand. The *brocanteurs* who remain are mostly gathered between the Periph and avenue de Bagnolet, with a motley assembly of none-too-clean jeans, carpenters' tools, holiday souvenirs, scuffed oil paintings, broken picture frames and shabby jackets hung up on the railings. Among the more hopeful items you find assorted household china, china oil lamps, vases, cast-iron casseroles, old records and a stand with old hi-fi units and electric guitars, alongside various objects (electric fuse boxes etc.) that you can't imagine anyone at all wanting and which may, perhaps, get packed up and shipped off to Africa. Among the impoverished local population, there are always a few hopeful outsiders, scouring the goods, but it's not really worth the trip, unless you're after a secondhand bike, perhaps, or an electric drill.

PUCES D'ALIGRE

Place d'Aligre, 75012
Tue-Sun mornings
Mᵒ Ledru-Rollin

The smallest of the official flea markets – and the only one right in central Paris – is a motley affair of piled up clothes, old prints and drawings, secondhand books, kitchen china and other miscellanea. It's junky but has a unique atmosphere nonetheless, with the noise and crowds of Paris' cheapest fruit and veg market alongside and the more exclusive delis, butchers and cheese stalls of the 19th century covered Marché Beauvais behind.

MARCHÉ AUX PUCES DE VANVES

Avenue Marc Sangnier, 75014
www.pucesdevanves.typepad.com
Sat/Sun 07:00-13:00
Mº Porte de Vanves

A small, genuine flea market that retains its appeal for treasure hunters, souvenir seekers and collectors, with a couple of hundred stands that spread out on tables or boxes on the ground under the trees on weekend mornings. There are lots of generalists, many with china, glass and small items, and a few specialists. The latter sell all manner of goods, including some great film posters with originals of Tati or a moody-looking Belmondo, old prints and postcards, advertising curios, jewellery (both costume and antique), fob watches, bundles of silver cutlery, clocks, antique cameras that go from old plate models to Polaroids, film projectors, small items of furniture, picture frames and decanters.

Prices vary widely: on some stalls the items cost a few euros; on others the prices rise into the hopeful hundreds. Throughout, the atmosphere is easygoing and relaxed, with a convivial mood as stallholders chat about their pieces or bargain gently. It's less for the big-budget collectors than St-Ouen but good for curios and souvenirs or items that are part of social history, such as old matchboxes, commemorative china or a stack of century-old handwritten menus for the *dîner du jour* at the Grand Hôtel in Nancy.

Vanves is small and manageable – if you arrive reasonably early you can just about get round the stalls in a morning. Note that this is a market that packs up early. The *brocanteurs* are out of here by 1pm, succeeded on Saturday by tawdry general goods and clothes stalls to be avoided.

MARCHÉ DU LIVRE ANCIEN ET D'OCCASION GEORGES BRASSENS

104 rue Brancion, 75015
01 42 50 80 25
www.gippe.org
Sat/Sun 09:00-18:00
M° Porte de Vanves or Convention

The antiquarian and secondhand book market held every weekend under the airy iron frame of an old livestock market on the edge of the Parc Georges Brassens is actually easy to combine with Vanves (see p126), only a ten-minute walk away. The 60 or so stalls vary slightly each week, but there are plenty of interesting niche specialities, from cookbooks to scandal sheets, philosophy or the history of Paris. There's a *braderie* twice a year when books are sold off for low prices, a weekend devoted to children's books and another to coincide with the Fête du Science in the autumn, attended by scientific book and instrument dealers from around Europe.

€ - €€

LES BOUQUINISTES

Right Bank, between Pont des Arts and Pont Louis-Philippe; and Left Bank, from Pont de Sully to Quai Voltaire
Daily 11:30–sunset
M° Saint-Michel, Pont Neuf or Pont Marie

The dark green boxes stretching along the Seine form part of the Parisian landscape, descendants of a centuries-old tradition of itinerant book and print sellers. Today, there are over 200 booksellers, 900 dark green boxes and an estimated 300,000 books making for a leisurely 3km stroll if you take in both sides of the river. Sadly, a few are more like souvenir shops, full of fridge magnets and reproductions of Parisian scenes and posters, but most remain dedicated to the secondhand tradition, as they unlock the boxes laden with books or piles of prints and lithographs. Many are enthusiastic specialists in anything from biography, war, crime, yachting, sociology and philosophy to advertising prints, fashion magazines or cookbooks.

BROCANTES & VIDE GRENIERS

Pretty much every weekend from April to October, you'll find a **brocante** stretching along some pavement in Paris. And it's often at these peripatetic *brocantes* that you come across the best finds. One of my favourites appears two or three times a year along Mouffetard (avenue des Gobelins) in the 5th arrondissement, where I seem to have picked up half the furniture in my flat. Similarly, the pitches around square du Temple in the 3rd or avenue des Ternes in the 17th are good, featuring well-vetted professional *brocanteurs* and traders who come up from the provinces.

Goods are incredibly varied but *brocantes* are often particularly good as a source of glasses and ceramics, piles of old dinner plates, old watches and jewellery, 50s and 60s furniture and big old country armoire wardrobes, 20th century industrial lamps, old station clocks, Bakelite instruments, postcards, lace and vintage fashion. Visit www.spam.fr (website of the Société Parisienne d'Animation et de Manifestation) for more on the city's *brocantes*.

Vide greniers are more like local jumble or car boot sales. The name means literally 'empty the attic', and these are very local affairs held out on the street, usually once or twice a year, when residents of a particular *quartier* pay a nominal fee for a few metres of space. *Vide greniers* are usually cheerful and convivial, and a good source of very cheap clothes, motley china, paperback books, DVDs and toys (an unimaginable numbers of Barbie dolls). See www.vide-greniers.org for listings of *vide greniers* and *brocantes* all over the city.

AUCTION HOUSES

Paris' homegrown auction system is a fascinating amalgam of the elite and the mundane, and although Sotheby's and Christie's have recently established premises here, it remains centred around France's unique system of *commissaires-priseurs* and Drouot, umbrella home for a multitude of auctioneers.

ARTCURIAL

7 rond-point des Champs-Elysées, 75008
01 42 99 20 20
www.artcurial.com
M° Franklin D. Roosevelt

Briest -Poulain-F. Tajan runs all sorts of auctions in this grand 19th century mansion on the Champs-Elysées, although has become particularly known for sales of wines, 20th century design and contemporary art, as well as specialist auctions that have included vintage Hermès and classic cars.

LE CRÉDIT MUNICIPAL

55 rue des Francs-Bourgeois, 75004
01 44 61 64 00
www.creditmunicipal.fr
M° Rambuteau

Behind a severe facade on one of the main Marais thoroughfares lies what is probably one of the oldest lending institutions in France, also known as Le Mont de Piété or *ma tante* (my aunt), alias the municipal pawnbroker. Founded in 1637 as a means to counter loan sharks, the current institution opened in the present address in 1778, and Parisians can still bring in a watch, wedding ring or other item here for a *prêt sur gage*. Items not reclaimed after a year are sold here at auction, with around a hundred public sales a year, especially of jewellery and silverware, although there are also sales of paintings, furniture, musical instruments and decorative arts.

DROUOT

9 rue Drouot, 75009
01 48 00 20 20
www.drouot.com
(see www.gazette-drouot.com for sale dates)
Mon-Sat 11:00-18:00 (closed mid-July to mid-Sept)
M° Richelieu-Drouot

Housed in a spiky 1970s monstrosity, where escalators take you up and down to 19 different red-carpeted salerooms, Drouot doesn't belong to a single auctioneer but stems from the specifically French system of *commissaires-priseurs*, with origins going back to 1552, who are both experts in antiques or collectables and have a legal qualification. There are literally thousands of sales each year, directed by over a hundred *commissaires-priseurs*, making this place an irresistible hive of activity, with viewings generally held the day before and on the morning of the sale. At any one time, you can flit between simultaneous sales and viewings that might take in old master paintings, general goods, fine wines, jewellery and watches, musical instruments, oriental antiques or vintage photos and posters. There's an incredible mixture of people and generations, professionals, collectors and mere addicts. A second branch, in the 18th arrondissement, is used for more everyday household stock, as well as (sometimes interesting) clearance sales of hotel and restaurant furnishings.

Other location
64 rue Doudeauville, 75018

CHARITY SHOPS

Parisian charity shops used to be rather desultory affairs full of unloved clothes, most of them linked to homeless charity Emmaüs, but there are signs of change with the well-selected clothes of the Secours Catholique's Bis Boutique Solidaire (see p17) and the smart new Oxfam bookshop (see p72). The other trend is for charity combined with recycling and job creation, as pioneered by Emmaüs Défi (see below) and the ressourceries. The three outlets listed here serve as a good taster for the Parisian charity shop scene.

€

L'APPARTEMENT EMMAÜS

Le 104 rue d'Aubervilliers or 5 rue Curial, 75019, La Villette
www.104.fr
Wed-Fri 15:00-18:00; Sat 12:00-18:00
(closed Aug)
M° Riquet

The bric-a-brac boutique at the colossal CentQuatre cultural centre – housed in the rehabilitated municipal undertakers – is entirely different from most of the Parisian shops run by Emmaüs, a charity founded in 1949 by L'Abbé Pierre to help the homeless. The clothes, furniture and objects are arranged as they might be in the rooms of an apartment, allowing you to bargain-hunt for a cause; some of the items are repainted, restored and customised by the crew of the Tribbu Déco social insertion project.

Nearby, in autumn 2012, Emmaüs Défi opened its largest charity shop yet inside the former Marché Riquet (36-42 rue Riquet; Sat 10:00-18:00), source of cheap secondhand clothes, furniture, household items and electrical goods, toys and books.

€

L'INTERLOQUE

7ter rue de Tetraigne, 75018
01 46 06 08 86
Mon-Sat 10:00-19:00 (closed 13:00-14:00)
M° Jules Joffrin

L'Interloque is part of the national network of *ressourceries*, which recuperate and recycle items, restoring and selling them on when possible, or sending off for recycling if not, while doubling as a social reinsertion job creation scheme and environmental awareness project.

MA RESSOURCERIE

3 rue Henri-Michaux, 75013
01 80 06 40 88
http://maressourcerie.fr
Wed 14:00-19:00; Fri 14:00-20:00;
Sat 11:00-20:00
M° Tolbiac

The shop run by the Studio-Carton association sells unwanted clothes, accessories, household china, lamps and small items of furniture, used books and electrical items. You can also take sewing lessons here or learn how to make cardboard furniture.

TROC AND ROLL

An alternative spirit of *troc*, or bartering, is bubbling under in the world of vintage, with convivial fairs where you can meet young creators or seek out bargains on vintage stalls, or take the chance to exchange books over an aperitif or brunch.

THE BOOK CLUB

Carmen, 34 rue Duperré, 75009
www.le-carmen.fr
M° Pigalle or Blanche
The monthly book swap at the stylish Carmen cocktail bar – in the grand *hôtel particulier* where Bizet lived while composing *Carmen* – is a hip version of the literary salon. Bring a book and exchange it for another one.

BRUNCH BAZAR

Cité de la Mode, 75013
www.wanderlustparis.com
M° Gare d'Austerlitz

An arty and alternative all-day open air market on the last Sunday of the month at the Cité de la Mode, with clothes from online vintage stores Dernier Cri Vintage and Freep'It, Shakespeare & Co bookstore (see p69), yoga, DJs, hamburgers from the Camion qui Fume, workshops and entertainment for kids and a huge outdoor terrace next to the Seine.

FASHION BRUNCH IN A CITY

Café A, La Maison de l'Architecture,
148 rue du Faubourg-St-Martin, 75010
www.inacity.fr
M° Gare de l'Est

A chilled out monthly rendezvous for gourmet brunch, young fashion creators and vintage clothes and accessories, held in the restaurant-gallery of the Maison des Architects in a renovated monastery near the Canal St-Martin.

LE FUMOIR

6 rue de l'Amiral Coligny, 75001
01 42 92 00 24
www.lefumoir.com
M° Louvre-Rivoli

This sleek, pared-back cocktail bar and brasserie (pictured left) facing the Louvre combines a jazz age speakeasy mood with a casual library at the rear. You can simply browse the literature, or bring in your own books to exchange for titles on the shelves.

TROC PARTIES

108 rue Oberkampf, 75011
06 25 75 03 49
www.le-bric-a-brac-bar.com
M° Rue Saint-Maur

Exchange or barter clothes, books and accessories two Saturday afternoons a month at the Bric-a-Brac Bar. See www.chacunsatribu.com for other *troc* events all over France.

Annual events for secondhand and vintage

LES PUCES DU DESIGN

Place des Vins de France, Bercy Village, 75012
www.pucesdudesign.com
Four days in May and Oct
M° Cour St-Emilion

The Puces de Design latched on early to the fashion for vintage furniture when it set up in 1999, before prices rocketed into the stratosphere, and after a few changes of address now seems to have settled in Bercy Village. Tightly focused on the 1950s to 90s, it's become a must for vintage design buffs, as almost a hundred dealers from Paris, the French provinces and all over Europe give the opportunity to discover pieces and designers you wouldn't find elsewhere, with a mix of exceptional design classics, mass-produced objects and quirkier items.

FOIRE NATIONALE À LA BROCANTE ET AUX JAMBONS

Pont de Chatou, Ile de Chatou
http://chatou.sncao-syndicat.com
Ten days in mid-March and late Sept
RER A St-Germain-en-Laye

Held on an island in the suburbs, this vast, eclectic fair has origins going back to the medieval Foire aux Lards, originally held in the city itself, and is still a curious, though rather fun, mix of flea market and food fair: browse through hundreds of antiques and bric-a-brac stalls and pause for ham, wine and charcuterie along the allée aux jambons.

SALON DU VINTAGE

**Espace d'animation des Blancs-Manteaux,
48 rue Vieille-du-Temple, 75004
www.salonduvintage.com
Three days each in May and Sept
Mᵒ St-Paul or Hôtel de Ville**

Established by vintage fanatic Laurent
Journo in 2008, this salon takes a pretty
loose definition of vintage, which means
that on one hand you might find a stall
stocked with almost entirely YSL and
Chanel, or another specialising in Paco
Rabanne and Courrèges, and on the other
find some pretty junky wear that is more
simply yesterday than vintage. You can
expect prices to vary wildly too. Clothes
and accessories are very much to the fore,
although there are usually a few stalls of
furniture, lighting and household items
and a specialist in old discs and record
players, along with a bar selling lemonade
and other retro drinks. Very popular
with vintage fashion fans, many of them
dressed to suit.

CARRÉ RIVE GAUCHE

**rue du Bac, quai Voltaire, rue de l'Université,
rue des Saints-Pères, 75007
www.carrerivegauche.com
Late May or early June
Mᵒ Rue du Bac or St-Germain-des-Près**

An annual open house for the smart
antique dealers of the 7th arrondissement
in the *carré* (square) of streets around
rue du Bac and quai Voltaire, with special
late and Sunday opening, when dealers
showcase an exceptional item.

BIENNALE DES ANTIQUAIRES

Grand Palais, avenue Winston Churchill, 75008
www.sna-france.com
Biennial (next event Sept 2014)
M° Champs-Elysées Clemenceau

One of the most prestigious antiques events in the world is home to leading international dealers in a stylish setting (designed in 2012 by Karl Lagerfeld) and it too has now embraced the 20th century alongside *grand siècle* antiques or *haute* jewellery. Classy, expensive and exclusive.

LE PAVILLON DES ARTS & DESIGN

Jardin des Tuileries, 75001
www.padparis.net
March
M° Tuileries

Held in a long white tent along the rue de Rivoli side of the Jardin des Tuileries, this is a fine and decorative arts fair, with the emphasis very much on 20th century design.

TOYMANIA

Palais des Congrès, place de la Porte Maillot, 75017
www.toymania.org
Biannual (June and Dec)
M° Porte Maillot

A toy collectors' fair featuring trains and robots, clockwork toys, dolls and cars from the 19th century to the 1970s.

CARTEXPO

Espace Champerret, place de la Porte
Champerret, 75017
www.cartexpo.fr
Two days in both Jan and May
M° Porte de Champerret

Huge vintage postcard fair with sellers
from all over France.

SALON DU LIVRE ET DES PAPIERS ANCIENS

Espace Champerret, place de la Porte
Champerret, 75017
www.joel-garcia-organisation.fr
One week in Oct
M° Porte de Champerret

Going strong since 1974, an incredible
biannual fair that takes in not just
antiquarian books but pretty much
anything on paper: posters, newspapers,
prints, postcards, playing cards, music
and photography, jam labels, bills or
stock actions.

PARIS
MAPS

The following collection of maps will help you navigate your way around Paris' secondhand and vintage shops and markets. Each corresponds to the zones used in the preceding chapters: Louvre and Les Halles; The Marais; Champs-Elysées and Passy; Montmartre, Pigalle and Batignolles; Bastille, Oberkampf and Canal St-Martin; Latin Quarter; St-Germain-des-Prés and Montparnasse; and Puces de Saint-Ouen (Clingnancourt). A final map, showing greater Paris and the city's arrondissements, marks all of the additional locations in Chapter Four.

Each entry is listed under its category and the colour of the icon on the map corresponds to that category, with sites marked by diamonds:

CLOTHES & ACCESSORIES

BOOKS, MUSIC & MEMORABILIA

HOME & INTERIORS

ONLY IN PARIS (SEE GREATER PARIS MAP)

A SELECT HANDFUL OF CAFES, BISTROS
AND BRASSERIES ARE MARKED BY A:

Each map has a QR code. If you have a smartphone, you can simply scan the code to link to online versions of the maps on Google which will help you find your way around. These maps are regularly updated to keep pace with Paris' evolving secondhand and vintage landscape.

LOUVRE/LES HALLES

Arrondissements 1 & 2

CLOTHES ◆
BOOKS & MUSIC ◆
HOME & INTERIORS ◆
BITES ◆
LANDMARK ★

CLOTHES

1 DIDIER LUDOT
20 and 24 Galerie de Montpensier,
Jardins du Palais-Royal, 75001
Mon-Sat 10:30-19:00

2 ESPACE KILIWATCH
64 rue Tiquetonne, 75002
Mon 14:00-19:45
Tue-Sat 11:00-19:45

3 FORGET ME NOT
90 rue de Richelieu, 75002
Mon-Fri 10:30-19:00

4 IGLAÏNE
12 rue de la Grande
Truanderie, 75001
Mon-Sat 11:00-19:00

5 LA MARELLE
25 Galerie Vivienne, 75002
Mon-Fri 10:30-18:30
Sat 12:30-18:30

6 NEILA VINTAGE
28 rue du Mont-Thabor, 75001
Tue-Sat 10:30-19:00

BOOKS & MUSIC

7 LA GALCANTE
52 rue de l'Arbre Sec, 75001
Mon-Sat 12:00-19:00

8 HIFI VINTAGE
9 rue des Déchargeurs, 75001
Mon-Sat 13:00-19:30

9 LIBRAIRIE DELAMAIN
155 rue St-Honoré, 75001
Mon-Sat 10:00-20:00

10 LIBRAIRIE GILDA
36 rue des Bourdonnais, 75001
Mon-Sat 10:00-19:00

11 LIBRAIRIE PARALLÈLES
47 rue St-Honoré, 75001
Mon-Sat 10:00-19:00

12 MONSTER MELODIES
9 rue des Déchargeurs, 75001
Mon-Sat 12:00-19:00

13 O'CD
24 rue Pierre Lescot, 75001
Mon-Sat 11:00-20:00
Sun 14:00-19:00

14 PARIS ACCORDÉON
36 rue de la Lune, 75002
Tue-Sat 10:30-19:00
(closed 13:00-14:30)

15 R.F.CHARLE
17 Galerie Véro Dodat, 75001
Tue-Sat 14:00-18:30

HOME & INTERIORS

16 GALERIE ALEXIS LAHELLEC
14-16 rue Jean-Jacques-Rousseau, 75001
Mon-Sat 12:00-19:00

17 L'OEIL DU PÉLICAN
13 rue Jean-Jacques-Rousseau, 75001
Tue-Fri 11:00-18:30
Sat 15:30-18:30

THE MARAIS
Arrondissements 3 & 4

CLOTHES ◆
BOOKS & MUSIC ◆
HOME & INTERIORS ◆
BITES ◆
LANDMARK ★

CLOTHES

1 LES ANTIQUITÉS DE L'ILE SAINT-LOUIS
20 rue des Deux Ponts, 75004
Mon-Sat 11:00-19:00

2 BIS BOUTIQUE SOLIDAIRE
7 boulevard du Temple, 75003
Tue-Sat 10:00-19:00

3 COIFFEUR VINTAGE
32 rue des Rosiers, 75004
Daily 11:00-21:00

4 DELPHINE PARIENTE
8 rue de Turenne, 75004
Mon 15:00-19:00
Tue-Sat 11:00-19:00
(closed three weeks in Aug)

5 FREE'P'STAR
8 rue Ste-Croix de la Bretonnerie, 75004
Mon-Fri 11:00-21:00
Sat-Sun 12:00-21:00

6 FRIP'IRIUM
2 rue de la Verrerie, 75004
Tue-Sat 13:00-21:00
Sun 14:00-21:00

7 HIPPY MARKET LE TEMPLE
21 rue du Temple, 75004
Mon-Sat 11:00-20:00
Sun 14:00-20:00

8 KING OF THE FRIP
33 rue du Roi de Sicile, 75004
Mon-Sat 11:00-19:30

9 MADE IN USED
36 rue de Poitou, 75003
Tue-Sat 11:00-19:30
(closed 14:00-14:30)
Sun 13:30-19:00

10 MAM'ZELLE SWING
35 bis rue du Roi de Sicile, 75004
Mon-Sat 14:00-19:00

11 MATIÈRES À RÉFLEXION
19 rue de Poitou, 75003
Mon-Sat 12:00-19:00
Sun 15:00-19:00

12 LE MONDE SECRET
21 rue St-Paul, 75004
Thur-Sun 14:30-18:30

13 ODETTA VINTAGE
76 rue des Tournelles, 75003
Tue-Sat 14:00-19:30
Sun 15:00-19:00

14 STUDIO W
6 rue du Pont-aux-Choux, 75003
Tue-Sun 14:00-19:30

15 LE VINTAGE BAR
16 rue de la Verrerie, 75004
Mon-Sun 11:00-20:00

16 VIOLETTE ET LÉONIE
27 rue de Poitou and 1 rue de Saintonge, 75003
Mon 13:00-19:30
Tue-Sat 11:00-19:30
Sun 14:00-19:00

BOOKS & MUSIC

17 ARCHIVES DE LA PRESSE
51 rue des Archives, 75003
Mon/Sat 14:00-19:00
Tue-Fri 10:30-19:00

18 INTEMPOREL
22 rue St-Martin, 75004
Tue-Sat 12:00-19:00

19 'CAMERA BOULEVARD'
boulevard Beaumarchais

20 LIBRAIRIE ULYSSE
26 rue St-Louis-en-l'Ile, 75004
Tue-Fri 14:00-20:00
(and occasional Sat)

21 MONA LISAIT
17bis rue Pavée, 75004
Daily 10:00-20:00

22 VIRTUOSES DE LA RÉCLAME
5 rue St-Paul, 75004
Tues-Sat 11:00-19:00

HOME & INTERIORS

23 **AU BON USAGE**
21 rue St-Paul, 75004
Wed-Mon 11:00-19:00

24 **AU PETIT BONHEUR LA CHANCE**
13 rue St-Paul, 75004
Thu-Mon 11:00-19:00
(closed 13:00-14:30)

25 **CASSIOPÉE**
Village St-Paul (in courtyard),
23-25 rue St-Paul, 75004
Thu-Mon 11:00-19:00

26 **AUX COMPTOIRS DU CHINEUR**
49 rue St-Paul, 75004
Tue-Sun 14:00-20:30

27 **GALERIE ANDERS HUS**
27 rue Charlot, 75003
Wed-Sat 14:00-19:00

28 **GALERIE BALOUGA**
25 rue des Filles du Calvaire
Tue-Fri 12:30-19:00
Sat 14:00-19:00

29 **GALERIE DANSK**
31 rue Charlot, 75003
Tue-Sat 14:00-19:00

30 **HIER POUR DEMAIN**
4 rue des Francs-Bourgeois, 75003
Tue-Sat 13:00-19:00
Sun/Mon 14:00-19:00

31 **MERCI**
111 boulevard Beaumarchais, 75003
Mon-Sat 10:00-19:00

32 **MOBILIER 54**
54-56 rue Charlot, 75003
Tue-Sat 11:00-19:00

33 **(RE)SOURCE**
7 rue de Turenne, 75004
Tue-Sun 11:00-20:00

BITES

34 **JAJA**
3 rue Sainte-Croix de la Bretonnerie,
75004

35 **CAFÉ CHARLOT**
38 rue de Bretagne, 75003

CHAMPS-ELYSÉES/PASSY

Arrondissements 8 & 16

CLOTHES ◆
BOOKS & MUSIC ◆
HOME & INTERIORS ◆
BITES ◆
LANDMARK ★

Quai Michele
Boulevard Bineau
Boulevard Pereire
Boulevard Pereire
Avenue de Villiers
Rue de Rome
Avenue Niel
Avenue de Wagram
Boulevard des Batignolles
Boulevard Pereire
Avenue des Ternes
Boulevard de Courcelles
Rue de Constantinople
Boulevard Malesherbes
Place de la Porte Maillot
Avenue de la Grande Armée
Avenue Mac-Mahon
Charles de Gaulle - Étoile
Boulevard Haussmann
Saint-Augus
Avenue de Friedland
Arc de Triomphe ★
Avenue Foch
Saint-Philippe-du-Roule
Miromesnil
Boulevard Malesherbes
Avenue Victor Hugo
Porte Dauphine
Kléber
Avenue des Champs-Élysées
Rue de Faubourg Saint-Honore
George V
Madelein
Avenue d'Iéna
Victor Hugo
Avenue Kléber
Avenue Marceau
Franklin D. Roosevelt
Avenue des Champs-Élysées
Rue Royale
Avenue Victor Hugo
Boissière
Champs-Élysées - Clemenceau
2
Rue de la Pompe
Grand Palais
Place de la Concorde
Concord
Avenue Georges Mandel
Iéna
Alma - Marceau
Cours Albert 1er
Cours La Reine
Voie Georges P
Quai des
Trocadéro
Avenue de New York
Avenue de New York
Quai d'Orsay
Voie sur Berge Rive Gauche
Quai Anatole Fr
Invalides
Avenue Rapp
Voie Georges P
1000ft
200m
1
3
Quai Branly
Avenue Bosquet
Boulevard de la Tour Maubourg
Boulevard des Invalides
La Muette
Rue de Passy
Passy
Tour Eiffel ★
Les Invalides ★
Avenue du Président Kennedy
Avenue Georges Pompidou
Allée des Cygnes
Bir-Hakeim
Avenue de Tourville
Quai Branly
Avenue de Versailles
Quai de Grenelle
Boulevard de Grenelle
Place Joffre
Boulevard des Invalides
Boule
Rue Frémicourt
Boulevard Garibald
Avenue Émile Zola
Rue de Sèvres
Rue
vres

CLOTHES

1 **DÉPÔT VENTE DE PASSY**
14 rue de la Tour, 75116
Tue-Sat 10:30-19:00

2 **RÉCIPROQUE**
89, 92, 93, 95, 97, 101
rue de la Pompe, 75016
Tue-Fri 11:00-19:00
Sat 10:30-19:00

3 **THE DATE**
3 rue de la Tour, 75116
Tue-Sat 11:00-19:00
(closed 14:00-15:00)

BOOKS & MUSIC

4 **ANTIQUE CAMÉRAS**
6 rue Miromesnil, 75008
Mon-Fri 11:00-18:00

5 **LIBRAIRIE D'ART ARTCURIAL**
7 Rond-Point des Champs-Elysées, 75008
Mon-Sat 10:30-19:00

MONTMARTRE/PIGALLE/ BATIGNOLLES
Arrondissements 9, 17 & 18

CLOTHES ◆
BOOKS & MUSIC ◆
HOME & INTERIORS ◆
BITES ◆
LANDMARK ★

Clichy

Quai Éric

Boulevard du Général Leclerc

Quai André

Quai

Quai Alphonse

Rue du Landy

Boulevard

Avenue C

Boulevard Victor H

Avenue Gabriel Péri

Rue de Rome

Quai de Clichy

Boulevard Jean Jaurès

Quai Grésille

Roquet

Boulevard Ney

Boulevard Ney

Ⓜ Porte de Clichy

Guy Môquet Ⓜ

Ⓜ Brochant

Avenue de Clichy

Avenue de Saint-Ouen

Jules Joffrin Ⓜ

Ⓜ Marcadet - Poissonn

Boulevard Ornano

Ⓜ Lamarck - Caulaincourt

Ⓜ d Berthier

Boulevard Pereire

15

Rue de Rome

1

Ⓜ La Fourche

6

Sacré-Coeur ★

Montmartre

Boulevard Barbès

Ⓜ Château Rouge

Wagram

Rue Lepic

4 **2**

Ⓜ Barbès - Rochechou

nue de Villiers

Ⓜ Rome

Place de Clichy Ⓜ

Boulevard de Clichy

10

Ⓜ Blanche

Ⓜ Abbesses

3

Boulevard de la Ch

Ⓜ Malesherbes

Boulevard des Batignolles

Ⓜ Pigalle

Boulevard de Rochechouart

Ⓜ Anvers

de Courcelles

Ⓜ Villiers

Rue de Constantinople

Pigalle

14

16 **17**

Rue des Martyrs

7

Ⓜ Gare du Nord

Rue de Rochechouart

Ⓜ Liège

Rue Blanche

18 **5**

3 **8**

Ⓜ Europe

) Wagram

Ⓜ Saint-Georges

Ⓜ Poissonnière

Ⓜ Notre-Dame-de-Lorette

Rue de Châteaudun

Rue La Fayette

Ⓜ Cadet

Boulevard Haussmann

Rue Saint-Lazare

Ⓜ Le Peletier

Ⓜ Saint-Lazare

Ⓜ Havre - Caumartin

Boulevard Haussmann

Ⓜ Chaussée d'Antin

13

12

Ⓜ Château d'Eau

Boulevard Malesherbes

Rue Scribe

Palais Garnier ★

11

Ⓜ Grands Boulevards

Boulevard de Strasb

Ⓜ Richelieu - Drouot

Boulevard Montmartre

mps-Élysées

Ⓜ Opéra

Ⓜ Quatre-Septembre

Ⓜ Bonne Nouvelle

Rue Royale

1000ft

200m

Avenue de l'O

Ⓜ Bourse

Rue Réaumur

Rue Saint-Martin

Avenue des Champs-Élysées

Cours Albert 1er

Cours La Reine

Voie Ge

ours Gauche

de Sébastopol

CLOTHES

1 BDA BASTIEN D'ALMEIDA
46 rue La Condamine, 75017
Tue-Sat 11:00-20:00

2 LA BOUTIQUE NOIRE
22 rue La Vieuville, 75018
Tue-Fri/Sun 14:00-19:30
Sat 11:30-19:30

3 CÉLIA DARLING
5 rue Henri Monnier, 75009
Mon-Sat 12:30-20:00

4 CHINE MACHINE
100 rue des Martyrs, 75018
Daily 12:00-20:00

5 FRIPES KETCHUP
8 rue Dancourt, 75018
Mon-Fri/Sun 14:00-20:00
Sat 11:00-20:00
(closed 13:00-14:00)

6 GUERRISOL
19 avenue de Clichy, 75017
Mon-Sat 10:00-19:30

7 MAMIE BLUE VINTAGE SPIRIT
69 rue de Rochechouart, 75009
Mon 14:30-19:30
Tue-Sat 11:30-19:30
(closed 13:30-14:30)

8 ZACH & SAM
13 rue Clauzel, 75009
Tue-Sat 10:30-19:30
(closed August)

BOOKS & MUSIC

9 AU TROISIÈME OEIL
37 rue de Montholon, 75009
Mon-Fri 13:00-18:00
Sat 12:00-16:00

10 LES CHEMINOTS + ASPHALTE
51 rue de Douai, 75009
Mon 14:00-19:00; Tue-Fri 11:00-19:00
Sat 10:00-19:00; Sun 11:00-18:00
(closed 12:30-15:00 (Sun only))

11 PASSAGE DES PANORAMAS
11 boulevard Montmartre,
10 rue St-Marc

12 PASSAGE JOUFFROY
10 boulevard Montmartre,
9 rue de la Grange-Batelière

13 PASSAGE VERDEAU
56 rue de la Grange-Batelière,
31 bis rue Montmartre

14 *RIFF ROW*

CENTRAL GUITARS
12 rue de Douai

LE GUITAR STORE
11 rue de Douai

LE GUITARIUM
9 rue de Douai

OLDIES GUITARS
31 rue Victor-Massé

15 VINTAGE GALLERY
17 boulevard Pereire, 75017
Tue-Sat 15:00-19:00

HOME & INTERIORS

19 **BROCANTE DES BATIGNOLLES**
16 rue Brochant, 75017
Tue-Fri 13:00-19:00
Sat 10:30-19:00

20 **CHEZ 1962/GALERIE 1962**
3 and 4 rue Tholozé, 75018
Tue-Sat 10:30-19:30

21 **DANK**
8 rue Bochart de Saron, 75009
Tue-Sat 13:00-19:30

22 **ET PUIS C'EST TOUT**
72 rue des Martyrs, 75009
Mon 14:00-19:00
Tue-Sat 12:00-19:30

23 **GALERIE CHRISTINE DIEGONI**
47ter rue Orsel, 75018
Tue-Fri 14:00-19:00
Sat 11:00-19:00

24 **MADAME CHOSE**
94 rue Nollet, 75017
Wed-Sat 11:00-19:30

25 **MOBILHOME**
106 rue Legendre, 75017
Tue-Sat 11:00-19:30

26 **L'OBJET QUI PARLE**
86 rue des Martyrs, 75018
Mon-Sat 13:00-19:00

27 **SPREE/PAPIERS PEINTS**
16 rue La Vieuville, 75018
Mon/Sun 15:00-19:00
Tue-Sat 11:00-19:00

28 **TOMBÉES DU CAMION**
17 rue Joseph-le-Maistre, 75018
Daily 13:00-20:00

29 **ZUT! FRÉDÉRIC DANIEL ANTIQUITÉS**
9 rue Ravignan, 75018
Wed-Sat 11:00-19:00
(closed 13:00-16:00); and Sun am

BITES

30 **MIROIR**
94 rue des Martyrs, 75018

31 **LES PUCES DE BATIGNOLLES**
110 rue Legendre, 75017

32 **HÔTEL AMOUR**
8 rue Navarin, 75009

CLOTHES

1 CHEZ CHIFFONS
47 rue de Lancry, 75010
Tue-Fri 11:00-19:00
Sat 13:00-19:00

2 COME ON EILEEN
16 rue des Taillandiers, 75011
Mon-Fri 11:00-20:00
Sat 14:00-20:00

3 DEBUT
28 avenue Laumière, 75019
Tue-Thu 10:00-19:30
(closed 13:00-14:00)
Fri 12:00-20:00
Sat 10:00-19:30
(closed 13:00-14:30)

4 LA MODE VINTAGE
12 rue Rochebrune, 75011
Fri/Sat 11:00-19:00; or by
appointment

5 OMAYA VINTAGE
29 rue Jean-Pierre-Timbaud, 75011
Mon-Sat 10:00-19:30

6 OPTIQUE DURABLE
2 rue Amelot, 75011
Tue-Sat 10:30-19:00
(closed 13:00-14:30)

7 THANX GOD I'M A VIP
12 rue de Lancry, 75010
Tue-Sat 14:00-20:00

BOOKS & MUSIC

8 BANCO CASH
37 boulevard Voltaire, 75011
Tue-Sat 10:00-19:00
(closed 13:00-14:00)

9 BIMBO TOWER
5 passage St-Antoine, 75011
Mon-Fri 13:00-19:00
Sat 11:00-19:00

10 BORN BAD
17 rue Keller, 75011
Mon-Sat 12:00-20:00

11 LULU BERLU
2 rue du Grand-Prieuré, 75011
Mon-Sat 11:00-19:30
(July-Aug 12:00-19:00)

12 MINIBUS
4 rue Monte Cristo, 75020
Wed-Sat 11:00-19:00 (closed Aug)

13 LES POUPÉES D'AUTREFOIS
116 avenue Parmentier, 75011
Mon-Fri 14:00-18:30 (or by
appointment)

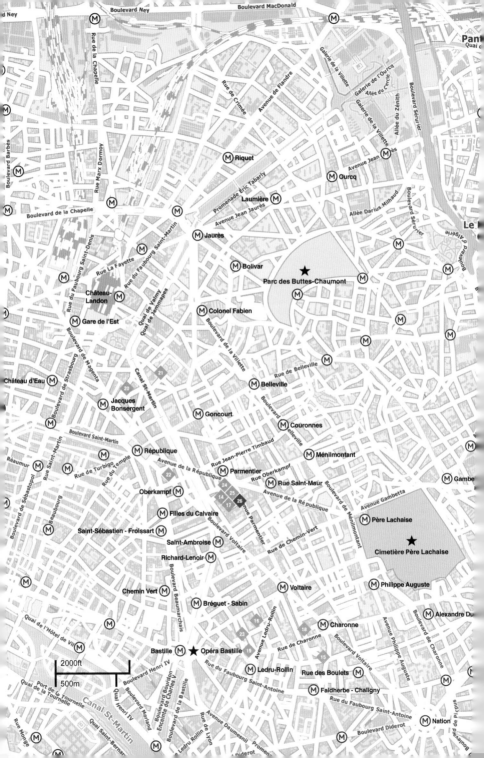

HOME & INTERIORS

14 **ALASINGLINGLIN**
1 rue du Marché Popincourt, 75011
Tue-Fri 12:00-19:00
Sat/Sun 14:00-19:00

15 **ANNA COLORE INDUSTRIALE**
7 rue Paul-Bert, 75011
Wed-Fri 13:00-20:00
Sat 14:00-20:00

16 **ATELIER BULLE**
8-10 passage Bullourde, 75011
Wed-Sat 11:00-19:00 (or by appointment)

17 **BELLE LURETTE**
5 rue du Marché Popincourt
Tue-Fri 12:00-19:00
Sat/Sun 14:00-19:00

18 **CAROUCHE**
18 rue Jean-Macé, 75011
Tue-Sat 11:00-19:00 (closed Aug)

19 **LE CHÂTEAU DE MA MÈRE**
108 avenue Ledru-Rollin, 75011
Tue-Sat 11:30-19:30

20 **COIN CANAL**
1 rue de Marseille, 75010
Tue-Fri 11:00-19:30
(closed 14:00-15:00)
Sat 11:00-19:30

21 **COLONEL**
14 avenue Richerand, 75010
Tue-Sat 10:00-19:00

22 **COMPLÉMENT D'OBJET**
11 rue Jean-Pierre Timbaud, 75011
Wed-Sat 15:30-20:00

23 **GALERIE PATRICK SEGUIN**
5 rue des Taillandiers, 75011
Mon-Sat 10:00-19:00

24 **PUDDING**
24 rue du Marché Popincourt, 75011
Wed-Fri 12:00-19:00
Sat/Sun 14:00-19:00

25 **RECYCLING**
3 rue Neuve Popincourt, 75011
Tue-Fri 12:00-19:00
Sat/Sun 14:00-21:00

BITES

26 **AL TAGLIO**
2bis Rue Neuve Popincourt, 75011

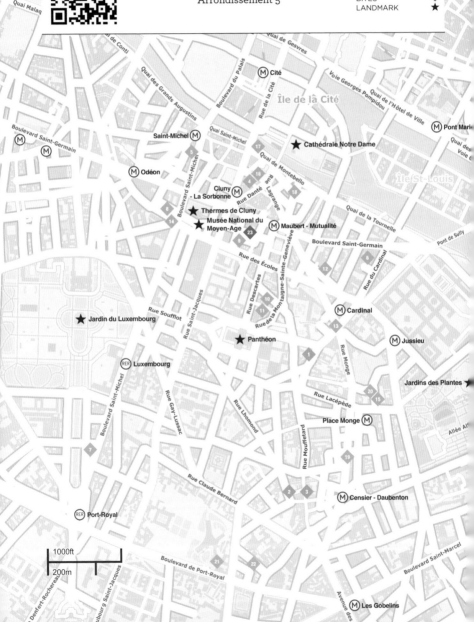

LATIN QUARTER
Arrondissement 5

CLOTHES ◆
BOOKS & MUSIC ◆
HOME & INTERIORS ◆
BITES ◆
LANDMARK ★

Georges Pompidou
Mitterrand

Quai Malaq

Quai de Conti

Quai des Grands Augustins

Boulevard du Palais

Quai de Gesvres

Ⓜ Cité

Voie Georges Pompidou

Quai de l'Hôtel de Ville

Île de la Cité

Rue de la Cité

Ⓜ Pont Mari

Quai des
Voie G

Boulevard Saint-Germain

Saint-Michel Ⓜ

Quai Saint-Michel

17

Quai de Montebello

★ Cathédrale Notre Dame

Île St-Louis

Ⓜ Odéon

Boulevard Saint-Michel

Cluny
- La Sorbonne Ⓜ

4 16

Rue Danté

Rue Lagrange

18

Quai de la Tournelle

Pont de Sully

★ Thermes de Cluny

9

14

★ Musée National du
Moyen-Age

23

5

Ⓜ Maubert - Mutualité

Boulevard Saint-Germain

8

Rue du Cardinal

Rue des Écoles

12

Rue de la Montaigne-Sainte-Geneviève

Rue Descartes

Rue Soufflot

10

11

Rue Saint-Jacques

Ⓜ Cardinal

13

★ Jardin du Luxembourg

★ Panthéon

Rue Monge

Ⓜ Jussieu

RER Luxembourg

1

Jardins des Plantes ★

Rue Lacépède

20

15

Boulevard Saint-Michel

Rue Gay-Lussac

Rue Lhomond

Ⓜ Place Monge

Allée A

7

19

RER Port-Royal

Rue Claude Bernard

2 3

Ⓜ Censier - Daubenton

1000ft

200m

Boulevard de Port-Royal

21

22

Boulevard Saint-Marcel

Avenue Denfert-Rochereau

Rue du Faubourg s Saint-Jacques

Avenue des Gobelins

Ⓜ Les Gobelins

CLOTHES

1 GÉNÉRIQUE
68 rue du Cardinal Lemoine, 75005
Mon 15:00-19:30; Tue-Sat 11:00-19:30
(closed 13:00-15:00)

2 LES MAUVAIS GARÇONS
10 rue de l'Arbalète, 75005
Tue-Fri 12:00-19:30
Sat 10:00-19:30

3 MICHEL WEBER ANTIQUITÉS BROCANTE
6 rue de l'Arbalète, 75005
Thu/Sat 11:00-19:00

BOOKS & MUSIC

4 AAAPOUM BAPOUM
8 rue Dante, 75005
Mon-Sat 11:00-20:00

5 ABBEY BOOKSHOP
29 rue de la Parcheminerie, 75005
Mon-Sat 10:00-19:00

6 L'AMOUR DU NOIR
11 rue du Cardinal-Lemoine, 75005
Daily 12:00-19:00

7 BOULINIER
20 boulevard St-Michel, 75006
Mon/Fri/Sat 10:00-00:00
Tue-Thu 10:00-23:00
Sun 14:00-00:00

8 CINÉ CORNER
1 rue de l'Ecole de Médicine, 75006
Mon-Fri 11:00-19:30; Sat 10:00-19:30

9 CROCODISC
40 and 42 rue des Ecoles, 75005
Tue-Sat 11:00-19:00 (closed Aug)

10 CROCOJAZZ
64 rue de la Montagne-
Sainte-Geneviève, 75005
Tues-Sat 11:00-19:00
(closed late July/early Aug)

11 LA DAME BLANCHE
47 rue de la Montagne-
Sainte-Geneviève, 75005
Mon-Sat 10:30-19:30; Sun 11:30-20:00

12 ETAT D'ORIGINE
5 rue St-Victor, 75005
Tue-Sat 14:00-19:00 (closed Aug)

13 GEPETTO & VÉLOS
59 rue du Cardinal-Lemoine, 75005
Tue-Sat 09:00-19:30; Sun 10:00-19:00
(closed daily 13:00-15:00; closed
Sun in Jan and Feb)

14 GIBERT JOSEPH
26-34 boulevard St-Michel, 75006
Mon-Sat 10:00-20:00

15 LIBRAIRIE MICHAEL SEKSIK
8 rue Lacépède, 75005
Mon-Sat 10:00-19:00

16 RACKHAM
2 rue Dante, 75005
Tue-Sat 10:00-20:00

17 SHAKESPEARE AND CO
37 rue de la Bûcherie, 75005
Mon-Fri 10:00-23:00
Sat/Sun 11:00-23:00

18 LA TORTUE ELECTRIQUE
7 rue Frédéric-Sauton, 75005
Tue-Sat 14:00-18:00

HOME & INTERIORS

19 AUX CÉRISES DE LUTÈCE
86 rue Monge, 75005
Mon-Sat 11:00-17:30

20 DANS L'AIR DU TEMPS
12 rue Lacépède, 75005
Tue-Sat 14:30-19:00 (closed Aug)

21 LILAS PORT ROYAL
72 bd du Port Royal, 75005
Mon-Sat 09:00-19:00

22 LUMIÈRE D'OEIL
4 rue Flatters, 75005
Tue-Fri 14:00-19:00
Sat 11:00-17:00

BITES

23 LE PRÉ VERRE
8 rue Thénard, 75005

ST-GERMAIN-DES-PRÉS/MONTPARNASSE

Arrondissements 6 & 14

CLOTHES ◆
BOOKS & MUSIC ◆
HOME & INTERIORS ◆
BITES ◆
LANDMARK ★

CLOTHES

1 **ADRENALINE**
30 rue Racine, 75006
Mon-Sat 11:00-19:00 (closed Aug)

2 **ALEXANDRA ZEANA**
19 rue de l'Echaudé, 75006
Mon-Sat 09:00-18:00
(closed 12:00-14:00)

3 **CHERCHEMINIPPES**
102, 109, 110, 111, 114, 124
rue du Cherche-Midi, 75006
Mon-Sat 11:00-19:00
(closed mid-July to mid-Aug)

4 **DÉPÔT VENTE DE BUCI BOURBON**
4 rue du Buci-Bourbon, 75006
Tue-Sat 11:00-19:00

5 **DOURSOUX**
3 passage Alexandra, 75015
Tues-Sat 10:00-19:30

6 **L'EMBELLIE**
2 rue du Regard, 75006
Tue-Sat 11:00-19:00

7 **LES GINETTES**
4 rue de Sabot, 75006
Tue-Sat 11:00-19:00 (closed Aug)

8 **KARRY'O**
62 rue des Saints-Pères, 75007
Mon-Sat 10:30-19:00

9 **MADAME DE...**
65 rue Daguerre, 75014
Tue-Sat 11:00-19:30
some Sun mornings
(closed mid-July to mid-Aug)

10 **LES TROIS MARCHES DE CATHERINE B**
1 and 3 rue Guisarde, 75006
Mon-Sat 10:30-19:30

BOOKS & MUSIC

11 **ANTIQ PHOTO**
16 rue de Vaugirard, 75006
Tue-Sat 14:00-19:00

12 **LA CHAMBRE CLAIRE/LIBRAIRIE CONTACTS**
14 rue St-Sulpice, 75006
Tue-Sat 11:00-19:00

13 **LA CHAUMIÈRE À MUSIQUE**
5 rue de Vaugirard, 75006
Mon-Fri 10:00-19:30
Sat 10:00-20:00
Sun 14:00-20:00

14 **CINE IMAGES**
68 rue de Babylone, 75007
Tue-Fri 10:00-19:00 (closed 13:00-14:00)
Sat 14:00-19:00 (closed Aug)

15 **LIBRAIRIE CINÉ REFLET**
14 rue Monsieur-le-Prince, 75006
Mon-Sat 13:00-20:00

16 **LIBRAIRIE LE PONT TRAVERSÉ**
62 rue de Vaugirard, 75006
Tue-Fri 12:00-19:00
Sat 15:00-19:00

17 **OXFAM LA BOUQUINERIE**
61 rue Daguerre, 75014
Tue-Sat 11:00-19:00
Sun 10:30-13:30

18 **PALEOPHONIES**
16 rue de Vaugirard, 75006
Tue-Sat 13:00-19:00 (closed Aug)

19 **UN REGARD MODERNE**
10 rue Gît-le-Coeur, 75006
Mon-Sat 11:30-20:00

20 **SAN FRANCISCO BOOK COMPANY**
17 rue Monsieur le Prince, 75006
Mon-Sat 11:00-21:00
Sun 14:00-19:30

HOME & INTERIORS

21 **LE CUBE ROUGE**
11 rue Lalande, 75014
Tue/Thu/Fri 13:00-19:30
Sat 10:30-19:30; Sun 10:30-13:30

22 **ESPACES 54**
54 rue Mazarine, 75006
Tue-Sat 14:00-19:00

23 **GALERIE DOWNTOWN**
18 and 33 rue de Seine, 75006
Tue-Sat 10:30-19:00
(closed 13:00-14:00)

24 **GALERIE JACQUES LACOSTE**
12 rue de Seine, 75006
Tue-Sat 11:00-19:00
(closed 13:00-14:00)

25 **GALERIE MATTHIEU RICHARD**
34 rue de Seine, 75006
Tue-Sat 10:30-19:00
(closed 12:30-14:00)

26 **JOUSSE ENTREPRISE**
18 rue de Seine, 75006
Mon 14:00-19:00
Tue-Sat 11:00-19:00

27 **LE PASSÉ D'AUJOURD'HUI**
43 rue du Cherche-Midi, 75006
Mon 15:00-19:00
Tue-Sat 10:00-19:00
(closed 14:00-15:00)

28 **LA SALLE DES VENTES
DU PARTICULIER**
117 rue d'Alesia, 75014
Daily 10:00-19:00

29 **SERENDIPITY**
81-83 rue du Cherche-Midi, 75006
Tue-Sat 11:00-19:00

30 **VELVET GALERIE**
11 rue Guénégaud, 75006
Tue-Sat 14:00-19:00

BITES

31 **LA PALETTE**
43 rue de Seine, 75006

32 **AGAPÉ SUBSTANCE**
66 rue Mazarine, 75006

PUCES DE SAINT-OUEN

ONLY IN PARIS
BITES

ONLY IN PARIS

1 **MARCHÉ VERNAISON**
99 rue des Rosiers/136 avenue
Michelet

2 **MARCHÉ BIRON**
85 rue des Rosiers

3 **MARCHÉ PAUL BERT**
96 rue des Rosiers or 18 rue
Paul Bert

4 **MARCHÉ SERPETTE**
110 rue des Rosiers

5 **MARCHÉ DAUPHINE**
138/140 rue de Rosiers

6 **MARCHÉ MALASSIS**
142 rue des Rosiers

7 **MARCHÉ JULES VALLÈS**
7-9 rue Jules Vallès

BITES

8 **LE PAUL BERT**
20 rue Paul Bert

9 **PIZZERIA LE NAPOLI**
136 rue des Rosiers

10 **CHEZ LOUISETTE**
130 avenue Michelet
(inside Marché Vernaison)

11 **LA CHOPE DES PUCES**
122 rue des Rosiers

THE ARRONDISSEMENTS OF PARIS

ONLY IN PARIS ◆

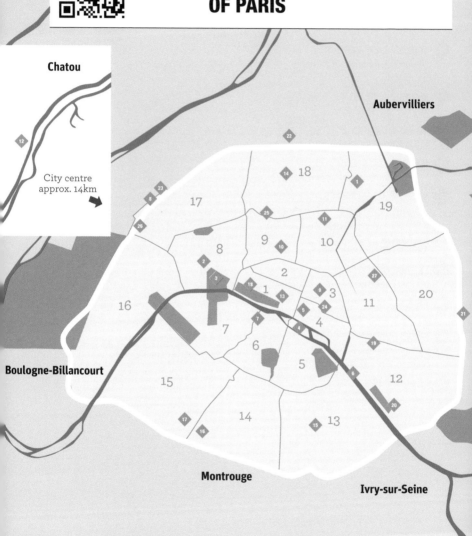

Chatou

Aubervilliers

City centre
approx. 14km

Boulogne-Billancourt

Montrouge

Ivry-sur-Seine

1 **L'APPARTEMENT EMMAÜS**
Le 104 rue d'Aubervilliers or
5 rue Curial, 75019
Wed-Fri 15:00-18:00
Sat 12:00-18:00 (closed Aug)

2 **ARTCURIAL**
7 rond-point des Champs-Elysées, 75008

3 **BIENNALE DES ANTIQUAIRES**
Grand Palais, avenue Winston
Churchill, 75008; biennial

4 **LES BOUQUINISTES**
Left Bank; Daily 11:30-sunset

5 **LES BOUQUINISTES**
Right Bank; Daily 11:30-sunset

6 **BRUNCH BAZAR**
Cité de la Mode, 75013

7 **CARRÉ RIVE GAUCHE**
rue du Bac, quai Voltaire, rue de
l'Université, rue des Saints-Pères, 75007
late May or early June

8 **CARTEXPO**
Espace Champerret, place de la Porte
Champerret, 75017; two days in Jan
and May

9 **LE CRÉDIT MUNICIPAL**
55 rue des Francs-Bourgeois, 75004

10 **DROUOT**
9 rue Drouot, 75009
Mon-Sat 11:00-18:00
(closed mid-July to mid-Sept)

11 **FASHION BRUNCH IN A CITY**
Café A, La Maison de l'Architecture,
148 rue du Faubourg-St-Martin, 75010

12 **FOIRE NATIONALE À LA BROCANTE
ET AUX JAMBONS**
Pont de Chatou, Ile de Chatou;
ten days in mid-March and late Sept

13 **LE FUMOIR**
6 rue de l'Amiral Coligny, 75001

14 **L'INTERLOQUE**
7ter rue de Tretraigne, 75018
Mon-Sat 10:00-19:00
(closed 13:00-14:00)

15 **MA RESSOURCERIE**
3 rue Henri-Michaux, 75013
Wed 14:00-19:00
Fri 14:00-20:00
Sat 11:00-20:00

16 **MARCHÉ AUX PUCES DE VANVES**
Avenue Marc Sangnier, 75014
Sat/Sun 07:00-13:00

17 **MARCHÉ DU LIVRE ANCIEN ET
D'OCCASION GEORGES BRASSENS**
104 rue Brancion, 75015
Sat/Sun 09:00-18:00

18 **LE PAVILLON DES ARTS & DESIGN**
Jardin des Tuileries, 75001; March

19 **PUCES D'ALIGRE**
Place d'Aligre, 75012
Tue-Sun mornings

20 **LES PUCES DU DESIGN**
Place des Vins de France, Bercy
Village, 75012; four days in May
and Oct

21 **PUCES DE MONTREUIL**
Avenue du Professeur
André Lemierre, 75020
Sat/Sun/Mon 07:00-19:00

22 **PUCES DE SAINT-OUEN**
Rue des Rosiers

23 **SALON DU LIVRE ET DES
PAPIERS ANCIENS**
Espace Champerret, place de la Porte
Champerret, 75017; one week in Oct

24 **SALON DU VINTAGE**
Espace d'animation des Blancs-
Manteaux, 48 rue Vieille-du-Temple,
75004; three days each in May
and Sept

25 **THE BOOK CLUB**
Carmen, 34 rue Duperré, 75009

26 **TOYMANIA**
Palais des Congrès, place de la
Porte Maillot, 75017; biannual
(June and Dec)

27 **TROC PARTIES**
108 rue Oberkampf, 75011

PARIS
INDEX OF SHOPS